A Guide To

The Queen Charlotte Islands

NEIL G. CAREY

ALASKA NORTHWEST BOOKS™

Edmonds and Anchorage

DEDICATION

To the Skidegate Mission and Haida families who
in 1955 with graciousness and dignity welcomed the four
Careys as open boat seafarers to share rest
on their shores and food on their tables.

First edition 1975
Ninth edition 1989

Library of Congress cataloging in publication data:
Carey, Neil G.
  A guide to the Queen Charlotte Islands.
  Includes index.
  1. Queen Charlotte Islands—Description and travel—
Guide-books.   I. Title.
F1089.Q3C33   1982   917.11'31044   81-12794
ISBN 0-88240-350-8   AACR2

CartoGraphics by Jon.Hersh

Alaska Northwest Books™
A Division of GTE Discovery Publications, Inc.
130 2nd Avenue S., Edmonds, Washington 98020
Printed in U.S.A.

Contents

A directory, listing the facilities available in the Queen Charlotte Islands (i.e., transportation, lodging, supplies), appears on the back of the color insert map included in this guide.

COVER — The Careys' converted lifeboat anchored in Blue Heron Bay. This maple leaf-shaped refuge on the west coast of Moresby Island is 9.5 kilometers south of Tasu Sound. This bay, nearly surrounded by abrupt sawtooth mountains, is sometimes subjected to violent gusts when the wind is from any southerly quadrant. The entrance is encumbered by rocks.

Foreword

Throughout World War II and the Korean conflict, the author, Neil G. Carey, was an officer in the United States Navy. After serving in Korea he resigned his commission and with his wife, Betty Lowman Carey, and their sons, George and Gene, set out to explore the Queen Charlotte Islands in a 19-foot Grand Banks dory. They followed the routes of the great Haida canoes that once ranged from the islands into Puget Sound.

Half a dozen years passed, but the Queen Charlotte Islands drew the Careys back. Betty and Gene made a trip in a dugout canoe along the west coast in 1962 and rediscovered the lagoon in which the Careys' cabin is now situated. The next year she and Neil rounded the islands aboard a British Columbia Forest Service vessel.

Neil G. Carey (John Wahl)

Meanwhile Neil had become a supervisor in the motion picture department of the Naval Missile Test Center, Point Mugu, California. In 1965 he resigned from that position to move to the Queen Charlottes. The Careys now have a year-round home at Puffin Cove, a hidden lagoon on Moresby Island's rugged west coast, and a town home in Sandspit, on the east coast.

Throughout the year the Careys explore, photograph and enjoy the islands, traveling by a 26-foot converted lifeboat in and out of every sound, inlet and bay. They have hiked along the drift of nearly every beach, followed many streams inland, climbed a few mountains, driven all the public roads and hundreds of kilometers of logging roads, and studied the islands from helicopters and small planes.

Neil has worked in the woods as a logger, flown and hiked with prospectors, toured the mines, participated in the fishing industry on boat patrol, accompanied sport fishermen, and taken North American, European, Asian and East Indian scientists to various remote spots in the islands.

The Charlottes' rugged west coast has been explored by Betty, in her precious 14-foot dugout canoe *BiJaBoJi*. Probably she is the last person to have enjoyed the abandoned Haida villages and ancient campsites on a dugout canoe journey.

The Careys have seen the islands' population grow from about 3,000 residents in 1955 to some 6,000 in 1989. During the intervening years mining towns and logging camps have come into being, served their purpose, and been torn down or moved.

Within the past few years the islands have been rediscovered. An ever-increasing number of tourists visit the islands, arriving by sea and air. Facilities at Sandspit Airport have been improved and expanded to accommodate those arriving or departing by air. Others, wishing to enjoy a short time at sea, or bringing their vehicle, will travel on the modern ferries *Queen of Prince Rupert* or *Queen of the North*. Clearly, a compact source of current information is needed for those who wish to see the unique Charlottes and for those who cruise by armchair.

The author has had articles and photos of the Queen Charlotte Islands in *ALASKA*® magazine and in *NORTHWEST EDITION*®, *Argosy*, *Canadian Geographical Journal*, *Travel*, *BC Motorist*, *Blackwood's* and other periodicals. He was selected to do the section about the Charlottes by the *Reader's Digest* for their book, *Scenic Wonders of Canada*. In late 1982 his book, *Puffin Cove*, was published, recounting some of the Careys' adventures in the Queen Charlottes.

—The Editors

THE METRIC SYSTEM

Canada uses the metric system. For convenience of U.S. visitors, distances in this guide are given both in kilometers and miles; temperatures, both in degrees Celsius and degrees Fahrenheit. Because distances given are approximate, both kilometers and miles have been rounded to the nearest half or whole.

Visitors to Canada can easily convert kilometers to miles by multiplying the number of kilometers by .62 or simply .6. Thus 100 kilometers equal 62 miles; 15 kilometers, 9 miles. 1 mile equals 1.6 km.

To convert from Celsius to Fahrenheit, double the degrees Celsius, subtract 10 percent of that number and add 32.

Gasoline is sold by the liter: 4.548 L = 1 Imperial gallon; 3.787 L = 1 U.S. gallon. Winter-Spring 1989 price of gasoline per Imperial gallon is $2.44 to $2.55.

The postal system is also metric and the minimum postage for letters or post cards is $.37 for 30 grams (28.35 grams = 1 ounce) within Canada, and $.43 for 30 grams to the United States.

CUSTOMS AND IMMIGRATION

Visitors from the United States may be asked to document their citizenship with birth, baptismal or voter's certificate.

Naturalized U.S. citizens should carry their naturalization certificates.

Permanent U.S. residents who are not citizens should have their alien Registration Receipt Cards with them.

Revolvers, pistols and fully automatic firearms are prohibited.

Dogs and cats from the U.S., if more than 3 months old, must be accompanied by a certificate signed by a licensed veterinarian of Canada or the U.S., certifying that the animal has been vaccinated against rabies during the preceding 36 months.

CURRENCY / CREDIT CARDS

Use of Canadian funds, in dollars or travelers checks, is recommended. Banks, credit unions or currency exchanges at Vancouver International Airport and the B.C. Travel Information Centre at the Douglas (White Rock) border crossing offer the prevailing rate of exchange. Major credit cards (Visa, MasterCard, American Express and others) are welcome in many Canadian businesses.

SEAT BELTS

It is mandatory in British Columbia that drivers *and* passengers use installed seat-belt assemblies while driving or riding in motor vehicles.

DRINKING AND DRIVING

British Columbia is waging constant war against impaired drivers. The risk of being caught is great; for even a first offense, penalties are serious.

TOURIST ALERT

The Royal Canadian Mounted Police are often asked to locate persons on vacation because of emergencies at home. There are TOURIST ALERT bulletin boards at many provincial campgrounds and Travel Information Centres, as well as radio messages.

Traffic Signs you will see when driving in British Columbia

REGULATORY SIGNS

STOP — YIELD RIGHT OF WAY — MAXIMUM 80 km/h — 50 km/h — TWO WAY TRAFFIC — KEEP TO RIGHT OF OBSTRUCTION

DO NOT ENTER — DO NOT PASS — PARKING PERMITTED AS INDICATED — SCHOOL CROSSING — TRUCK ROUTE — NO HEAVY TRUCKS — NO STOPPING

NO LEFT TURN — NO RIGHT TURN — TURN LEFT — TURN RIGHT — NO TURNS — NO U TURNS — PARKING PROHIBITED

WARNING SIGNS

STOP AHEAD — SIGNALS AHEAD — SLIPPERY WHEN WET — BUMP AHEAD — STEEP HILL — TWO WAY TRAFFIC AHEAD

ADVANCE SCHOOL CROSSING — ADVANCE PEDESTRIAN CROSSING — PLAYGROUND AHEAD — DIVIDED HIGHWAY ENDS — PAVEMENT ENDS — DEER CROSSING

PAVEMENT NARROWS — CREW WORKING — SURVEY PARTY AHEAD — NARROW STRUCTURE — RAILWAY CROSSING — CURVE AHEAD

INFORMATION SIGNS

HOSPITAL — AIRPORT — TELEPHONE — CAMPING SITE — PICNIC SITE — SANI-STATION — HOTELS MOTELS

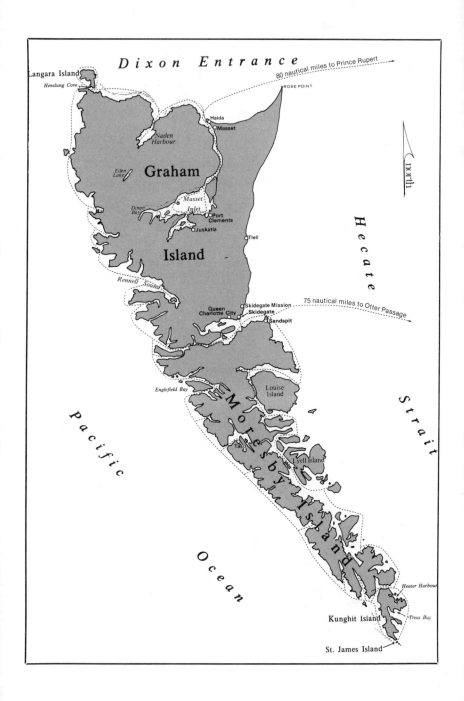

Introduction To The Queen Charlotte Islands

To the sailor or fisherman plying the Inside Passage to Alaska the Queen Charlotte Islands exist only as names on his chart, for this archipelago of some 150 islands and islets lies far out of sight of the regular lanes of travel. The islands are much like coastal British Columbia and Alaska — but in miniature. Here mountain peaks reach to less than 4,000 feet, and the fjordlike inlets are only 8 kilometers (5 miles) long rather than 10 times that.

The Charlottes, as they are called by some 6,000 residents, consist of six main islands, Langara, Graham, Moresby, Louise, Lyell and Kunghit, grouped in a rough triangular shape 250 kilometers (156 miles) long and 85 kilometers (52 miles) wide at the point of greatest width. Moderated by a countercurrent of the great *Kuroshio* (Japan Current), the islands have an annual average temperature of 7.8°C (46°F), with only 53.4 inches of annual rainfall on the east side of the mountains — despite slanderous rumors of continual downpours.

Though they lie between 52° and 54° North Latitude — as do Dublin, Amsterdam and Berlin — the Charlottes are peacefully removed from the crush of all but major world events.

On the islands' northernmost point the Langara Island lighthouse winks at Cape Muzon, Alaska, 29 miles distant, on the other side of Dixon Entrance. In spring, summer and fall these waters, rich with salmon, halibut and crab, are speckled with the boats of commercial and sport fishermen. The commercial fishermen deliver their catches to the cannery at Masset or to Prince Rupert, or to buying boats that transport the fish to mainland canneries or freezing plants.

Archaeologists estimate that the Charlottes have been inhabited for more than seven thousand years. Petroglyphs similar to those at Wrangell have been discovered on Lina Island. Who were those ancient artists?

Haida Indians were here in 1775 to greet the first European explorers on record. Those Haidas, soon renowned for their distinctive wood carvings and their lavish potlatches, and as hunters of the sea otters whose rich furs were prized by traders sailing on to China, were quickly devastated

1

These modern passenger and vehicle ferries serve the Queen Charlotte Islands. The 332-foot Queen of Prince Rupert *(foreground) maintains five trips weekly between the mainland port of Prince Rupert and Skidegate on Graham Island, June through September. During the other months the 410-foot* Queen of the North *makes the crossing thrice weekly.* (British Columbia Ferry Corporation)

by diseases common to Europeans. Their abandoned villages can be seen along the coast. Today most Haidas live on reserves at Skidegate Mission and Haida, on Graham Island. (See insert map.)

Graham Island, the largest of the Charlottes, was the first to attract white settlers. These pioneers came to the low, flat east coast and to the shores of Masset Inlet, in the island's center. Today Graham Island — home for four out of every five islanders — has 12 villages, settlements and camps, most of them connected by good blacktopped road. Outlying logging camps at Eden Lake, Tartu Inlet, Naden Harbour, Dinan and McClinton bays are reached by boat, amphibian plane or helicopter.

In the fall of 1980 a new all-tides ferry dock was completed at Skidegate, on Graham Island, and in mid-November the 332-foot MV *Queen of Prince Rupert* commenced scheduled runs between Prince Rupert and Skidegate, a distance of 93 nautical miles. This modern, 18-knot ship — part of the British Columbia Ferry System — has a capacity of 90 vehicles and 430 passengers and, in summer, makes 5 round trips weekly (3 in winter), taking approximately 6-8 hours for each crossing.

A year-round schedule is maintained between Prince Rupert and Skidegate, thence to Port Hardy. Storms may delay but rarely cancel a sailing. In summer — June through September — these routes are served by the *Queen of Prince Rupert* and the larger *Queen of the North* — 410 feet long, carrying up to 95 vehicles and 750 passengers. This comfortable ship has 95 staterooms. One accommodates wheelchairs.

In summer the trips between Prince Rupert and Port Hardy are 15-hour day cruises through the spectacular Inside Passage; north one day, south the next.

2

Symbolizing the Haidas who were the first inhabitants of the Queen Charlottes, this weathered totem peers from the encroaching forest at Ninstints, an abandoned village on Anthony Island Provincial Park, also a world heritage site.

On the winter schedule — October through May — the *Queen of the North* or the *Queen of Prince Rupert* takes both runs: three round trips between Prince Rupert and Skidegate each week, and one between Prince Rupert and Port Hardy, stopping at Bella Bella for passengers only.

As one crewman told me, "If it's legal on the road, the *Queens* can carry it."

Getting any place is part of the fun, so make the "Totem Circle" — north on Vancouver Island to Port Hardy, then by comfortable ferryliner to Prince Rupert and across to the Charlottes. Homeword bound, see Prince Rupert and Prince George before turning south through British Columbia's always changing interior to Vancouver or Seattle. It's a year-round route, over good highways. You may want to reverse the route, or, in Prince Rupert, board an Alaska state ferry and explore the Last Frontier. (See *The MILEPOST®*)

Board at Port Hardy, pick up the key to your stateroom at the purser's office — if you want this extra comfort; then relax and enjoy the next 15 hours as you cruise through 274 nautical miles of the spectacular Inside Passage. Thrill to the ever-changing scenes of the majestic, tree-covered coastal mountains, and pass isolated waterfront settlements, logging areas, lighthouses, fishing vessels, barges piled high with great logs, and guess the destination of tugs with heavy tows bound for distant ports, before disembarking at Prince Rupert. (All passengers and vehicles must get off at Prince Rupert, reboarding 2 to 4 hours later.) Take two or three days to visit the bustling seaport of Prince Rupert, or board for the crossing to Skidegate where you begin days, or weeks, of exploring the Charlottes. Reservations are strongly recommended.

Friendly, helpful personnel make riding the *Queen of Prince Rupert* or *Queen of the North* a genuine pleasure. The cafeteria serves good meals at moderate prices. Staterooms or dayrooms are available. Ship-to-shore-telephone, a well-stocked gift shop, an elevator to promenade and boat decks, and facilities for the disabled are some of the comforts of these fine vessels. Numerous large windows offer views of superb land- and seascapes whether one is enjoying a filling meal in the spacious dining room, relaxing or reading in comfortable chairs inside or on deck, or studying a chart and making plans in the well-stocked bar. Land is within sight at all times during clear weather.

Graham Island is close abeam to starboard after your ferry has crossed Hecate Strait and entered the deepwater channel of Skidegate Inlet near Lawn Point. Scattered homes are sighted among wind-tried trees behind beaches of wave-washed rock and coarse gravel. Soon the interesting Haida village of Skidegate Mission comes into view, surrounding open, crescentic Rooney Bay and climbing the gentle hillside. A tall totem marks the village offices. Torrens and Jewell islands are passed before your memorable sea trip ends at the dock in Skidegate and your drive or hike to new adventures in the Queen Charlottes commences.

The 235-foot Kwuna *makes frequent daily crossings of Skidegate Inlet, going from Alliford Bay to Skidegate. The ferry can carry 25 vehicles and 150 passengers on the scenic 20-minute trip.*

Sandspit — site of the island's jet airport, a radio station, and a logging camp of the Crown Forest Industries Ltd.

Hecate Strait was calm on most of our many crossings. We find the ferry a pleasant and economical means of travel to and from the mainland, or to Vancouver Island for the scenic drive to Victoria. But when it's rough . . .

Reservations are recommended. (See TRANSPORTATION, FERRIES in the Recreational Directory.)

MV *Kwuna*, a 235-foot ferry, was put into service in 1975 and runs between Alliford Bay, on Moresby Island, and Skidegate, on Graham Island. Based at Alliford Bay, the *Kwuna* has a capacity of 25 cars and 150 passengers, and makes frequent scheduled crossings between 7:00 A.M. and 10:30 P.M. daily. Foot passengers can usually catch a ride into town.

The 20-minute trip across the bay affords a spectacular view of Skidegate Inlet, Bearskin Bay and a glimpse of Haina, the now overgrown site of an abandoned Haida village on Maude Island. Fishing boats, pleasure craft and powerful ocean-going tugs with log barges are frequently seen and photographed in these protected waters. (See TRANSPORTATION, FERRIES in the Recreational Directory on the back of the insert map.)

From Alliford Bay a 14-kilometer (9-mile) road curves along the shores of Skidegate Inlet, crossing small salmon streams and passing through stands of spruce, hemlock and cedar before reaching Shingle Bay and Sandspit.

Sandspit Airport, about 18 feet above sea level, has a 5,120-foot runway and is the only port of entry for aircraft in the Charlottes. The airport has all facilities for travelers, and there are daily jet flights between Sandspit and Vancouver. In addition, amphibious planes make daily flights

5

between Masset, Sandspit and Prince Rupert. (See TRANSPORTATION, AIR in the Recreational Directory.)

The logging camps at Sewell Inlet and Beattie Anchorage (on Louise Island) are serviced by both scheduled and charter flights, as are the settlements and camps on Graham Island.

On Kunghit Island a small number of private homes have been built at the site of the old Rose Harbour whaling station. This low, forested island was once used by the Haidas for summer camps. There are lovely crescent beaches of golden sand at the head of open bays on the island's southeast and southwest sides; catchalls for interesting ocean drift. Heater Harbour, on the northeast side, and Rose Harbour, on the north, provide the seaman with mooring buoys and all-weather shelter.

The beaches and beachcombing are two of the major reasons for visiting the Charlottes. Among the finds on Graham Island one year were the jaw, skull and ribs of a small whale. Betty Carey, wife of the author, is holding the jawbone.

Lonely Cape St. James, on St. James Island, where a crew of three maintain the meteorological station and lighthouse, lies at the southern tip of the Charlottes. In 1787 Capt. George Dixon named both the island and the cape after rounding them in his ship *Queen Charlotte* on St. James's Day.

Many visitors to the Charlottes arrive at Sandspit by jet aircraft from Vancouver. From a window seat your first glimpse of the islands may be the bent-thumb-shaped land beneath you, the site of the airport and the seaside settlement of Sandspit. This spit, between Hecate Strait and Shingle Bay, is the largest area of flat land on Moresby Island and home for nearly 600 people.

Over half the settlement's working population is involved in some phase of logging. Others work at the airport, at the radio station, or in services. Local services include grocery, general, sporting goods, and variety stores, a hotel, gift shops, cafes, garage-service station, heavy equipment repair shop, car rental agencies, amphibious plane, helicopter, and boat charters, RCMP officer, post office, aviation fueling facilities, taxis, hunting and fishing outfitters, golf course, and retail liquor agency. Service clubs are Lions International, Rod and Gun Club, and Alcoholics Anonymous.

Two commercial vehicles meet the incoming and departing forenoon flights of Canadian Air International. One transports passengers to and from Queen Charlotte City. The other transports freight to the major settlements on Graham Island. Renting a vehicle, hiring a taxi or depending upon friends are at present the only means of getting to Masset or intermediate villages. CAI's daily evening flights — four nights weekly in winter — are not met. (See TRANSPORTATION, BUSES, in the Recreational Directory.)

If you prefer to rent a vehicle you may do so at the airport while waiting for your luggage to be unloaded, or you can pick one up in Queen Charlotte City, Skidegate or Masset.

Cafes, hotels and motels are located in Sandspit, Queen Charlotte City, Port Clements and Masset.

Bed and Breakfast accommodations are proliferating in most communities. Current information may be obtained from Joy, operator of the Travel INFOCENTRE (605-559-4742) at Joy's Island Jewellers (open every day) halfway between the ferry docks and Queen Charlotte City (an excellent source of Haida-crafted argillite, gold and silver, island-related books, souvenirs).

For the vacationer or explorer who arrives in the Queen Charlotte Islands aboard his own vessel, or who brings a pneumatic boat and outboard, or a good kayak, a long list of recreational possibilities exists. Fuel capacity is the only limiting factor — assuming that you have time to wait out any storm. Marine fuels are available only in Masset, Port Clements, Skidegate on Graham Island, and, by truck, in Sandspit on Moresby Island. (See SHOPS & SERVICES, MARINE FUELS in the Recreational Directory.) Rivulets along steep cliff sides will keep your freshwater tank full. Just bring a garden hose and funnel.

A sailor's best investment, after a seaworthy hull and reliable engine, is the $125 spent to acquire a complete set of charts covering the Queen

Charlotte Islands; *Sailing Directions, British Columbia Coast (North Portion);* and a tide book to keep him or her informed of that 26-foot tidal range. It is also a good idea to carry extra anchors and plenty of line or chain. Storms can make safe anchoring difficult in some areas, and mooring buoys can be crowded with four to six boats at each buoy.

The islands' location, configuration and supply sources are such that if one crosses Hecate Strait from Prince Rupert or Banks Island, landing at Masset, it is convenient to cruise the Charlottes in a figure-eight course. Prevailing winds are from the northwest and southeast.

Whatever the mode of transportation, no one should try to fit the islands into a rigid schedule. Adverse weather can delay or cancel commercial flights and sailings for a day or so. Small planes or vessels may have to wait a few days for fog to clear or winds and seas to quiet.

NATURAL HISTORY

The Charlottes, which are on the average 96 kilometers (60 miles) from the mainland, lie on the edge of the continental shelf. To the east is shallow Hecate Strait, 50 to 300 feet deep; to the west the shelf plunges deep into the Pacific only a mile or two offshore.

This is Canada's most active earthquake area. Scientists read a long history of geological violence in local rocks, for the Queen Charlotte Islands were once intruded, uplifted and folded until, looking like a marble cake frosted with lava, they were broken open, glaciated and eroded. The Charlottes' hillsides are scarred by slides, many initiated by seismic activity and/or heavy rainfall. The high peaks are often bare of vegetation and snow-covered. Slopes above the treeline are frequently decorated with alpinelike meadows.

Deer add a gentle touch to the Charlottes' scenery. This fawn greeted the author from the shelter of a leaning totem at the abandoned Haida village of Ninstints.

Blacktail deer were introduced to the Charlottes a century ago as a ready meat supply. With abundant forage, a mild climate and no natural predators, they have prospered and are found on all the islands. These deer are not difficult to hunt, are smaller than their mainland cousins and provide delicious venison. (See FISHING & HUNTING in the Recreational Directory.)

Drivers may encounter these lovely animals day or night. I always enjoy the sight of a doe or fawn bounding along a treelined road, or an old buck — white rump flashing, belly swaying like a hammock — following my route until he disappears into a hidden roadside trail. But be warned that blacktails sometimes make what appear to be suicidal dashes in front of vehicles, a disaster to both.

During the late spring and early summer you may discover a tiny spotted fawn lying still along the roadside, in the grass, or on a lonely beach. It is not abandoned; just hiding. Soon after you depart, its mother will return to feed and care for this cuddly creature that you may be tempted to "help," or claim as a pet — which is illegal.

Other introduced animals — the elk, raccoon, squirrel, beaver and muskrat — continue to expand their numbers and their range each year.

Black bears are often seen on all major islands. Some attain greater size than most mainland blacks. So far none of these bears have attacked people, but be wary.

You may be lucky enough to see a sleek-furred river otter romping along a stream, tobogganing down a muddy slope, or fishing in some sheltered bay. These thick-bodied, long-tailed animals are the subspecies *Lutra canadensis brevipilosus*, the Queen Charlotte otter.

At one time the islands had an indigenous animal, the dwarf, mouse-gray Dawson caribou, but it became extinct more than a half-century ago.

The islands have several subspecies of birds and plants. Bird watchers may encounter some difficulty in identifying birds on the Charlottes, for many indigenous birds tend to be darker than their mainland counterparts. Subspecies of three birds, the saw-whet owl, the hairy woodpecker and the Steller's jay, are found only in the Charlottes. A subspecies of the pine grosbeak is found here and on Vancouver Island, while a subspecies of the song sparrow is here and on Alaskan islands. In addition, you will spot a few lazy or storm-battered migrants that have stayed to enjoy the islands' mild climate.

The Steller's jay was voted British Columbia's official bird in 1987. The peregrine falcon came in a close second. This jay is often seen around bird-feeders, heard chattering in scrub trees and rose bushes, or glimpsed in the sheltering coniferous forest. This intelligent, friendly — if you supply food — bird, with black foreparts and long crest and deep blue body, wings and tail, is a worthy addition to Canada's provincial birds.

No matter how you travel or where you go on the Charlottes, you will see bald eagles. The magnificent adults are unmistakable, their white heads and tail plumage contrasting sharply with their dark brown, nearly black bodies. Immature birds are brown, mottled with white, until their fourth or fifth year, and are sometimes mistaken for golden eagles. An isolated point, a tall gray snag or a high windswept rock is the location preferred

Adult and immature bald eagles perched high above Tasu Sound.

by eagles for their lookouts. In late summer and early fall eagles flock to streams where salmon are spawning. At any time of year you can hear the eagles' high-pitched squeaks and rapid, sharp chirps, or see them soaring on wings that span over 6 feet. Their nests, in large trees and generally miles from civilization, often look like misplaced piles of brush.

Indigenous plants include six mosses and liverworts that exist only in the Charlottes; in addition, there are others known only here and in Japan or in western Europe.

The waters surrounding the Charlottes abound with life and activity. Commercial fishing season begins when seiners and gillnetters congregate during March and April to compete with sea lions, seals, porpoises and great flocks of sea birds for the roe-filled herring. Halibuters, salmon trollers and seiners work around the islands until late September or early October, when the season is closed — after the streams have been filled to capacity with spawning salmon. For the sportsman there are still a few late-arriving salmon, returning steelheads, and the always-present trout and Dolly Vardens. Hardy fishermen using hundreds of traps to catch Alaska black cod (sablefish) labor offshore nearly year-round.

Whale-watching is popular in late spring and early summer as gray whales, migrating from the warm lagoons of Baja California to the chill waters of the Bering Sea and Arctic Ocean, pause to feed in Skidegate Inlet. As the gray whale population increases, so do the numbers seen here. More than 26 were counted in the inlet in 1988, the first in April and the last in late June. They may be sighted singly or in small pods, bottom-feeding on amphipods in shallow water.

Scan the inlet for the blow — water or condensing vapor — rising as high as 12 feet as the whale exhales. Once seen, you should see it again, or another, perhaps a cow and calf. They may make short dives and frequent blows, or they may stay down for several minutes.

In the summer, rafts of vellela, a sail jellyfish 2½ to 3½ inches long, cover the sea surface and sometimes number in the hundreds of thousands. When washed ashore they look like snow, and are slippery as ice. In mid-summer, yachtsmen may be startled by what appears to be an uncharted reef ahead but is really a dense collection of moon jellyfish. These are about 6 inches in diameter and drift at or just below the water's surface in quiet bays or inlets. Sea blubbers, large jellyfish up to 20 inches in diameter, are frequently seen in the open ocean or drifting with the tide in the bays. They remind me of monstrous raw eggs.

WEATHER

For those interested in checking the weather situation before deciding what type of clothing to pack for a trip to the Charlottes, here are a few figures based on observations taken over a period of 25 years at Sandspit and Masset.

Average temperature during coldest month, January	1.7 °C (35 °F)
Average daily maximum during January	4.2 °C (40 °F)
Average temperature during warmest month, August	14.5 °C (58 °F)
Average daily maximum during August	17.8 °C (64 °F)
Average annual temperature	7.8 °C (46 °F)

Fishing in the streams and bays of the Charlottes is excellent. Here a father and son show their morning catch of lingcod. These fish were taken on a jig. Although not much for fighting, lingcod are choice eating.

11

Maximum recorded temperature	28.9°C	(84°F)
Minimum recorded temperature	-18.9°C	(-2°F)
Average precipitation during wettest month, October	201mm	7.9"
Average precipitation during driest months, May-Aug	58mm	2.3"
Total annual precipitation	1356mm	53.4"
Maximum recorded rainfall in one day	80mm	3.1"
Number of days a year with precipitation		213
Number of days a year with snowfall		18
Number of days a month with fog		2

CLOTHING

Dress in the islands is generally informal. The same outdoor wear you would pack for an excursion to Vancouver Island, the Inside Passage, Puget Sound, coastal Oregon or northern California is appropriate — something in light- to medium-weight wool, a waterproof lightweight jacket (brightly colored for pictures) and comfortable, waterproof walking or hiking shoes.

Fleet's in! Trollers, seiners and gillnetters flock to the Charlottes during the salmon season, filling the protected moorage at Queen Charlotte City.

FILM

Most stores carry a variety of film for still cameras in color, black and white and Polaroid. (Most 35mm color film sold in Canada includes processing charges with purchase price.) A few stores have 8mm color film. Anyone who uses a 16mm movie camera, sheet film or video recorder should bring an adequate supply.

In any case, plan on doubling your usual amount of shooting, whether you specialize in people, nature, landscapes, seascapes, rainbows, sunrises or sunsets. Each scene in the Charlottes acquires a subtle contrast as the time of day changes or the background of billowing clouds in a rich blue sky becomes charcoal gray because of distant and probably approaching showers. Spectacular crashing waves, close-ups of wildlife and your prized fish catch will also use up your film.

CAMPING

Camping along one of the fishing streams or on a secluded beach is a pleasant and inexpensive way to explore the islands. Nearly all streams have trout and, depending upon the time of year, may have salmon or steelhead. With a rod and reel your meal is no farther away than the nearest stream.

Although the Charlottes have few organized campgrounds, there are miles of accessible public beaches, and camping or overnight parking is usually permitted in the inactive parts of tree farms. A drive or hike along almost any unused logging road will soon bring you to an enticing camping spot. Do you prefer your views to be gentle or rugged? Streams, mountains, forest or sea — you can choose a campsite that will give you a view of these or any combination.

Open campfires are a hazard in the woods. Save your campfires for the beach — but not amid the drift logs. The British Columbia Forest Service requires that a shovel and two-gallon container of water be on hand for extinguishing campfires.

ATTRACTIONS

REGIONAL MUSEUM: Skidegate Mission

The attractive wooden structure of the Queen Charlotte Islands Regional Museum overlooks Second Beach near Skidegate Mission on Graham Island. Haida totems and argillite carvings are displayed here plus settlers' relics, natural history exhibits and photographs of the Haidas and other early residents. In this centrally located museum residents and students learn of the past, while tourists may begin an acquaintance with these out-of-the-way islands.

THE ED JONES HAIDA MUSEUM: Haida

This museum is located on a knoll near the north side of Haida, where it overlooks the community recreation field and a few recently carved totems. Numerous Haida artifacts are attractively displayed here.

PORT CLEMENTS MUSEUM

Newest of the island's museums — opened in 1987 — is on the water-front side of the town's through road. It specializes in local logging, mining and fishing industry displays. Photographs, old equipment, household items and other well-identified treasures will acquaint you with the pioneers.

LOGGERS DAY: Sandspit

Each year on a Saturday in late May or early June, loggers from throughout the Queen Charlotte Islands, the mainland, and Vancouver

Island gather in Sandspit to compete for prizes awarded for a number of industry-related contests and to determine the winner of the handsome King Logger Trophy. It's a day of excitement when the men come out of the bush to demonstrate the many skills required in their trade.

Cameras click as husky men in plaid shirts take part in the fast-action birling contest. A pair of men leap onto a floating log, their caulked boots digging in like claws as each man — using his weight and a skillful sense of balance — tries to spin the log, first in one direction and then, after a fast stop, in the other direction, until one man is caught off balance and splashes into the chill water. "Next contestants, please!"

For the climbing contest, tree climbers strap on their irons, cinch thick leather safety belts and race, squirrellike, up an 80-foot pole to ring a bell mounted at the top. Seventy seconds is a good time for this exhausting event for the high-riggers. For safety men are timed only on the climb, not the round trip, so they no longer plummet to the ground.

Next, their axes honed to razorlike sharpness, loggers await the signal to start swinging in the horizontal- and standing-chop events. Axes bite deep with a musical ring, and wedge-shaped chips fly. In a matter of moments the winner has made a smooth cut through an alder log.

Chain saws, snapping and snarling, are tested one more time as the beginning of the bucking contest nears. "Start!" With a deafening noise the sawing begins. Blades drop onto the log and sawdust jets out as the carefully filed chains slash through the wood. It's over in a minute or so and the saws are shut off. The log is now only a row of blocks and piles of yellow sawdust.

Birling contest during Loggers Day. Despite the soaking the losers get, there are always plenty of contestants for this test of skill on rolling logs.

Other events include choker setting (connecting a heavy wire strap around one end of a log that is lying on the ground), obstacle bucking, wire splicing and a tug of war.

One of the most spectacular events is the ax throw, in which hurled axes spin toward a target marked on the butt of a large log.

There are events for the ladies, too: birling, choker setting, peavey logrolling, bowline tying and nail driving. To the winner goes the Queen Logger Trophy. Boys have a choker setting contest.

Refreshments are available throughout the day, as are various games of skill for visitors of all ages. There is no admission charge.

LOGGERS DAY: Port Clements

During an August weekend, Port Clements conducts a Loggers' Sports Day at an old homestead just west of town. Another chance to cheer for your favorite contestant, or just watch the exciting display of loggers' skills.

THE WILLOWS GOLF COURSE: Sandspit

This popular nine-hole course in Sandspit is part of a pioneer homestead along the shores of Hecate Strait. It is open year-round, weather permitting, which in the mild climate of the Charlottes might mean golfers can work off the overstuffed feeling that follows a Christmas or New Year's dinner. During the long summer days, players can often be seen enjoying the course until after 10:30 P.M.

Sand traps, natural water hazards, groves of trees and fairways totaling 3,000 yards result in a course with a par 36 for men and par 39 for women. The course has 18 tees and provides enjoyment for good golfers and a workout for duffers. Refreshments are available at the clubhouse, where carts and clubs can be rented and balls and tees replaced.

Each August the Willows Open, a mixed tournament, attracts contestants from the western provinces and the Pacific Northwest. (See SHOPS & SERVICES, GOLF in the Recreational Directory for address.)

DIXON ENTRANCE GOLF and COUNTRY CLUB: Masset

This lovely golf course lies in the rhythmically rolling dunes between the blue waters of Dixon Entrance and the road from Masset to Tow Hill. The Dixon Entrance Open, a pleasant and challenging event, is held each August.

COHO SALMON DERBY: Sandspit

Four weekends in September and October (which ones depend upon weather and the timing of the salmon runs) have a special attraction for fishermen: the Sandspit Rod & Gun Club Annual Coho Derby. Resident and visiting entrants try for the big coho (silver salmon) of the Charlottes, competing for an array of prizes and trophies awarded in four categories. A small entry fee is required.

Trophies are awarded for (1) the largest coho caught by anyone with an entry ticket, (2) the largest coho caught by an entrant under age 14, (3) the coho caught by the youngest contestant and (4) the largest coho caught by a woman ticketholder.

For a person to be eligible for prizes, the coho must be taken in the area between the Deena River and the south point at Gray Bay during any of the derby weekends.

To win the big prize, a fisherman will probably have to get a coho of over 16 pounds and usually the winner must land a salmon in excess of 18 pounds. One year the prize-winning coho weighed in at more than 24 pounds.

There are free boat launching sites at Copper Bay, Sandspit, Alliford Bay, and at the head of Cumshewa Inlet.

FAMILY TROUT DERBY: Mosquito Lake

Late in May the Sandspit Rod & Gun Club sponsors a Family Trout Derby at Mosquito Lake. Camping spots along the shoreline are claimed by many who wish to be in the middle of the action and also enjoy the beauty of snow-draped mountains; others camp in secluded nooks in the second-growth forest, while a few commute from home. Trophies are awarded to lucky anglers of all ages. There also is a prize for the largest trout and a trophy for the youngster landing a trout winning the hidden-weight award.

SINGAAY LAA: Skidegate Mission

This Haida "Good Day" celebration, in early June, is a fine way to see Haida regalia, sample many Haida foods, and enjoy water and shore sports and competitions.

HOSPITAL DAY: Queen Charlotte City

This annual celebration is held on a Saturday in late June. It includes a colorful parade, numerous races afloat and ashore, softball games, water skiing, helicopter rides, arts and crafts displays, concessions and, of course, lunch and dinner to sustain visitors through this day-long event, concluding with a dance. This festival was originated 69 years ago as a fund-raiser for the islands' hospital.

CANADA DAY: Port Clements

On the long First of July weekend, Port Clements hosts a full program of events for all ages. Activities from Friday evening through Monday evening include a parade, softball tournament, pole climb, Yakoun River "yacht" race, games of chance, movies, pancake breakfasts, salmon barbecue and chicken dinners, and a Saturday evening dance.

COUNTRY FAIR: Tlell

This fair is held at the Tlell fairgrounds, across from the Naikoon Park headquarters, in midsummer. Start in the morning with an ample pancake breakfast at the Bellis Lodge. Inspect the exhibits of livestock, vegetables, flowers and home preserves. Go to the park headquarters to see movies (free) shot in various parks. Try your skill, or luck, in the fishing derby, trap shoot or logger sports. See it all from the air on a short helicopter ride. Neither rain nor wind deters islanders from flocking to this popular event, concluded with a barbecue supper.

HUNTING, FISHING, CRABBING AND MOLLUSK GATHERING
(See FISHING & HUNTING in the Recreational Directory for license information.)

HUNTING

These are your hunting possibilities: *Big Game:* black bear, blacktail deer and elk; *Small Game:* raccoon; *Game Birds:* blue grouse; *Water fowl:* ducks, geese and black brant.

Deer hunting is excellent throughout the islands, though most animals are smaller than mainland deer and trophy racks are difficult to find. There is little gamy flavor in this tender and delicious venison.

Black bear hunting is unexcelled and there is a good chance of taking a mature animal having a skull of record proportions.

A black bear and cubs: a sample of the Charlottes' supply of big game.

Only a few elk are taken each year. Elk are a challenge to the hunter's skill and patience. One young islander told me proudly of taking a fine bull elk on the season's opening, and the many tiring trips to pack out the meat.

Blue grouse hunting is fair, varying from year to year.

Waterfowl hunting is superior throughout the many bays, inlets and grassy flats. Black brant hunting is outstanding.

FISHING

Perhaps fishing is the most popular sport of the islands because it is done amidst beautiful surroundings. In the Charlottes fishing is a year-round

A pleased fisherman displays what he plans to have for dinner. Although coho are the favorite catch of salmon fishermen, pink salmon (shown) also provide good sport and excellent eating.

sport combining the best of freshwater and saltwater angling with an opportunity to land a big one if you're going after chinook (spring/king) and coho (silver) salmon or steelhead. In the past logging sometimes took place right to the water's edge. But now a green belt is left along the streams or beaches. Birds nest in the green belt, deer browse, and trees cool the streams while also helping to control the occasional superabundance of fresh water.

The gradient of most of the Charlottes' fishing streams is such that at high tide the streams are full for a kilometer or more inland from their mouths. Streams are posted to mark the end of tidal fishing.

What's your pleasure? Will it be an unforgettable contest with 18 pounds of fighting coho; or the pleasant if less spectacular catching of a string of cutthroat, rainbow trout and Dolly Varden to cook over the campfire; or the excitement of tangling with an 8- to 30-pound steelhead? Or is it going to be a quiet morning in a small boat jigging for lingcod, red snapper, rockfish or halibut — perhaps a halibut so large it cannot safely be brought aboard? Or will you slip into scuba gear and search out the small, delicious pinto abalone or purple-hinged rock scallop — they grow up to 10 inches in diameter; or will you laze around camp until the tide is nearly out, then grab your trusty clam gun and dig a meal of razor clams?

All of this is possible in the Queen Charlottes and, with the exception of salmon and steelhead fishing, can be enjoyed at any time of year.

Chinook salmon show up in Hecate Strait in late April and begin entering some of the inlets. Chinooks are taking lures or bait herring in Tasu Sound by early May. Coho usually appear about a month later, increasing in size and numbers while they feed and slowly migrate to the streams of their origin until late September or early October, when coho fishing is at its height.

In season, a number of sports-fishing charter boats and lodges operate in the Charlottes. Chinook salmon fishing usually begins around Langara Island in April. Some boats follow the salmon down the west coast of

Graham Island during the summer and end the season fishing coho in Moresby Island's Cumshewa Inlet during August and September.

Small boats, motors, fishing tackle, rain clothes (when needed), life jackets, catch care for those 30- to 60-pound chinooks, and air fare from Vancouver, B.C., are included in the package price.

The precise time when coho school up off the mouths of streams varies, sometimes resulting in great fishing in one area and poor sport only a few kilometers away. Anyone fishing from late August to mid-October has a good chance to catch the limit. (Be sure to check local fishing regulations for current information on limits and licenses.)

Pink salmon are frequently caught, chum salmon occasionally, and sockeye salmon rarely, in tidal waters (they're illegal in nontidal) from mid-August to early October. While not as large or such fierce fighters as coho or chinook salmon, they do add variety to the sport and are choice for smoking, an art the Haida Indians have perfected.

November through April is when the wily, fighting steelhead trout flourish in the streams, providing a real challenge for the experienced fisherman, whether fly casting or drift fishing. A steelhead is an anadromous rainbow trout that has spent from one to four years in salt water growing large, independent and combative before returning to its native stream to spawn. Unlike all Pacific salmon, a steelhead does not necessarily die after spawning.

Cutthroat and rainbow trout and Dolly Varden are taken year-round. They always put up a good fight and are delicious to eat whether cooked over an open campfire or at home.

Those who have fished salmon, steelhead and trout know what combination of rod, reel, line, lures and action is most successful. Those who haven't should be aware that this kind of fishing is something like training a dog: You have to be wiser and have more tricks than the dog.

Rods most often seen along the streams, shores, or in boats are six to nine feet long, of medium flexibility, strong and mounted with noncorrosive guides and fittings. Spinning reels are most popular and usually loaded with 6- to 16-pound-test monofilament line. Occasionally a sportsman will test his skill with lighter line and a limber rod. Those who will not chance losing a precious salmon often use 20-pound test. Whatever, keep the hook needle-sharp and untarnished.

In addition to flashers and spinners, leaders, swivels and weights, you will need a selection of lures including a couple sizes each of Krocodiles, Kit-a-mat, Mepps Aglia, Comet, and Black Fury, Dardevles, Buzz-Bombs, teespoons, colorful bucktails and dry and wet flies. As one of my more successful salmon-catching friends once advised, "Also buy anything else that looks pretty."

There is no guarantee that anything will work. I have been with ardent, experienced fishermen who flogged the streams and salt water all day without so much as a strike. Worse, we could see hundreds of 10- to 16-pound cohos darting about in the shallow water and two or three jumping near us at any time. On other days, the ones best remembered, a coho will strike a lure on the first cast and not be seen until it rockets into the air attempting to shake the hook — and the fight is on!

Those with larger boats may have good sport trolling in Hecate Strait from Skincuttle Inlet to the north of the Tlell River, or in Dixon Entrance from Massett Harbour to the north and east sides of Langara Island, or through Skidegate Channel into Cartwright Sound. Or work over the rocky bottom of Cartwright Sound for lingcod and halibut. On reasonably calm days, many persons fish along the sharp drop-off of the extensive spit from Sandspit northward to the buoys marking the Skidegate shipping channel. Fishing is best when the tide is running, especially during the flood tide when small fish are swept over the bar where feeding salmon are jumping and splashing.

Fishermen in skiffs and small boats may feel more comfortable in the protected waters of the inlets and bays on the east coast of Moresby Island, in Skidegate Inlet, or near the entrance to Masset Harbour.

Try a 16-ounce weight about four to six feet ahead of a flasher trailing a hootchy-kootchy-type lure on a 24- to 30-inch leader, or use a lighter weight and tie on a headless herring impaled on tandem hooks, either 1/0 or 2/0. One hook is usually placed sideways near the tail and the other shoved upward through the herring's backbone. If the tide is running you may be able to just drift and work this bait. Keep that dip net or gaff within reach.

Nearer the stream mouths or in the small bays, you might elect to cast, either from shore or the boat. Nearly all metal lures of assorted shapes and colors have their advocates. The one thing most favorites have in common is a touch of red someplace. There are days when a Kit-a-mat is the hottest lure; other days it will be a Mepps Aglia #3, or perhaps a Krocodile. During two seasons I fished with a party that had fished all over the world. One used only a Dardevle. She didn't waste time digging in her tackle box or changing lures. She just fished. At the end of each trip she had caught as many salmon or trout as anyone in the party, and her 18-pound, 12-ounce coho tied for largest fish. The other big one was caught trolling with a 2-ounce weight ahead of a green and white bucktail.

Waders and a sturdy dip net or gaff should be included in your gear, although I have seen a few 12- to 18-pound cohos caught by fishermen wearing street shoes while standing on rocks in back eddies. Such a fisherman would skillfully fight the fish to exhaustion before slipping a finger inside the gill cover and proudly carrying the prize up the beach.

September, when the greatest numbers of fishermen are in the Charlottes and when hotel reservations and boat and vehicle rentals are the tightest, can be a month of cloudless days when one wears sunglasses and fishes with sleeves rolled up. These are days when mallards and assorted ducks dabble and dive nearby, bald eagles ride the thermals, and the salmon lie offshore in cool tidal water waiting for the streams to rise sufficiently so they can enter and spawn. When the rain comes, the fish charge upstream. It is often a time of frustration and disappointment for the angler without a boat or for the fisherman who cannot wait for the salmon to make their dash. Once headed for the spawning grounds, the salmon may strike angrily at any bright metal spoon cast before them.

September can also be a month when one wild rain-pelting southeaster follows another with only a few hours of letup in between. At such times

Winter steelhead fishing in the Queen Charlotte Islands can become addictive. The weather, although often wet, is not especially cold, but there is competition for the best fishing holes.

soggy fishermen cast or troll in dark, roiled waters. Often such a fisherman will be rewarded by the slamming strike of a heavy coho that rips off yards of monofilament before somersaulting into the air, crashing into the water and starting a long, rod-bending run. Yes, the ducks are still there, getting ready for their migration, but the eagles are now perched on upper limbs of trees, watching for the next meal to swim by.

Usually September is a month of mixed weather. There's enough rain to fill the streams and allow the salmon to go into the shallows on flood tides, then drift out with the ebbs until ready to make a leisurely trip to the spawning beds. Those are the days you should catch your limit, whether fishing from the beach or a boat.

Salmon runs in some of the Charlottes' streams have been enhanced by private and government efforts. The first returns came to one of those streams in the fall of 1987. Hundreds, perhaps thousands, of adult coho salmon worked their way along the shores of Shingle Bay to their home stream, finning and leaping and attracting eager fishermen.

Local and visiting fishermen found superb sport for weeks, especially during the two hours before and two hours after high tide. Men in chest-waders stayed dry as they followed the run across the gently sloping tide flats parallel to Sandspit's Beach Road. On two successive days I saw a young man, on his lunch break, wade in up to his chest, cast a bright spoon, and soon tie into a lively 10- or 12-pound coho. Not many places you could do that!

On one bright, calm September day, two of us in a Boston whaler dashed out to Skidegate Channel. As we came out of the West Narrows we saw salmon leaping near the mouth of Government Creek. The tide was nearly high, and hundreds of pink salmon were flitting over the gravel shoals.

Cohos often swim quietly amidst such excitement.

After a few casts with a dressed Mepps Aglia #2, I was fighting a scrappy pink, and in about five minutes I brought an exhausted fish aboard. Bill, my experienced companion, was soon playing his first pink salmon. Within a half hour we landed three more of those tasty five- to six-pound fish.

Too soon the tide turned, and thousands of pinks started out of the stream in splashing schools. Hundreds at a time churned the water into riffles, as if it were flowing over a bouldered bottom. We sat in the boat, then stood ashore, our fishing rods ignored, watching as some dozen waves of salmon sought the deeper saltwater. Memory of that sight will linger long after the thrill of the catch is forgotten.

If you have never seen salmon spawning, it is a sight worth the loss of a few hours' angling. Follow a stream inland and watch the pinks, which spawn before the cohos. They will skitter and flop across rocky shoals, their backs out of the water, then rest in small quiet pools. By now their tails and fins are battered and damaged. Then they will again move onward, perhaps leaping over an obstructing tree trunk where the water swirls and churns, until they come to a place with clear water running over fine gravel where, with swift, violent movements of her skinned tail, the female excavates a small hollow area. Her hook-nosed, hump-backed mate hovers nearby, belligerent and eager to chase off other males. Satisfied, the female settles over the shallow hole and deposits the dark pink eggs. Then the male covers them with the fertilizing milt. Exhausted, both scatter gravel and sand over the redd (the nest), hiding the precious eggs that would attract hungry trout and voracious Dolly Varden, or be washed downstream to the waiting gulls.

Spawned out, the male and female drift away to die. The next hard rain may flood the valley floor. When the stream recedes to its bank, in a day or so, the grassy floor of the forest will be littered with dead salmon; a feast for eagles, gulls, ravens, crows and black bears fattening up for the winter.

October is often a month of heavy rainfall and violent winds. Streams rise overnight, their waters swift and roiled. Determined salmon drive upstream. At these times some fishermen quickly land their limits; others fly home disappointed.

The winter run of steelhead enters the streams early in November to spend the winter teasing hardy fishermen before spawning in late winter or early spring and then drifting back to the ocean. By May the steelhead are just memories — the kind that fish stories grow from.

There is a small summer run of steelhead in one or more of the short streams gushing into Tasu Sound, and it is possible that others exist, since some of the less accessible west coast streams have not had more than a cursory prospecting.

None of the island streams are more than a few miles long. Among the favorites are Yakoun, Tlell, Mamin, Hiellen, Chown, Copper, Deena and Pallant; all accessible by road. These streams have holding pools where the fish rest, feed and perhaps strike lures on their passage upstream.

Many of the local steelhead are high-jumping, slashing runners weighing 8 to 14 pounds. The larger ones, up to 30 pounds, are sometimes compared to big chinook salmon, and the fight a steelhead gives you may well last over half an hour — if the tricky creature doesn't tangle the line in some underwater snag and escape. You will discover that local streams have numerous obstructions, some attributable to old logging practices but most of them natural windfalls, that are too heavy to be flushed out by spring or fall freshets. These often work to the advantage of the fish.

A majority of the steelheaders with big rods and reels are spin fishermen who drift their lures or bait suspended two or three feet below a cork bobber. (Roe is a favorite bait.) Often a fisherman will plunk his or her own special lure, carefully weighted with pencil lead or maybe with only a 3/8-ounce silverspoon, into a pool, or cast quartering upstream and allow the lure to bounce down the riffles. Plenty of spare lures, hooks, leaders, sinkers and bobbers are necessary due to hidden snags and low overhanging branches.

The steelhead sometimes tendermouth the bait, too often undetected, rather than slam in with a fierce strike. Experts claim it's the cold water that causes the fish to do this.

One of the local guides became a catch-and-release fan one day when he couldn't drop a hook into the stream without a steelhead darting away with it. Before that memorable afternoon was over he and a companion had landed and quickly released 36 fighting steelhead. "It was a once-in-a-lifetime experience," he told me, still amazed by their luck.

Will the skillet be large enough? The author with an 80-pound halibut caught on a jig. A boater equipped with a jig on a long hank of 200-pound test line is sure to catch plenty of lingcod, red snapper and halibut.

23

Lures are usually available in local stores. Sometimes the selection becomes pretty well picked over late in the season and all the hot lures are gone. So bring your favorite lures and buy some local favorites, just to be sure.

Offshore or in most bays and inlets you might try jigging for lingcod, red snapper, assorted rockfish, and the choice halibut. A halibut may be large enough to straighten your hook and escape; otherwise it will put up one terrific tail-flopping fight before being subdued and boated. This is a fun way of catching a good meal, though generally not considered sport fishing. The jigger (usually a bright three-sided metal lure, slightly curved, weighing 6 to 21 ounces and often fitted with triple hooks) is tied up to a 50- to 200-pound test monofilament line and dropped to the bottom then worked by hand in lively jerking movements that raise the lure from the bottom two or three feet each time. A pair of light gloves is helpful.

Kelp patches or bottoms of sand, gravel or small rocks are generally recommended as places to go for lingcod, red snapper, rockfish and halibut. Find on your chart the seamounts or banks that rise above the surrounding deeps, then locate them with a depth finder or hand lead or by triangulation. Fishing is usually best when the tides are moving and carrying feed past these bottom fish.

CRABBING AND MOLLUSK GATHERING

Crabbing is especially good on the sandy bottom along the northeast coast of Graham Island where Dixon Entrance and Hecate Strait meet. This is the area where commercial boats set their heavy traps for Dungeness crabs. These catches are sold to the freezing plant in Masset or flown to Vancouver. Other places for crabbing are Masset Inlet, Naden Harbour and Security Cove. Waste fish or a punctured can of sardines is good bait. Prawns or shrimp are taken in Masset Inlet, Naden and Thurston harbours, Tasu Sound, Skincuttle Inlet, and other bays and inlets.

A variety of edible mollusks are found along the islands' shores. Best known locally and most sought after is the delectable razor clam, dug for commercial and personal use in the sand beaches of the north and east coasts of Graham Island. These are great in chowders or roasted on a stick over a campfire. (Check locally for season and limit.)

Butter clams, littleneck clams, soft-shell clams, horse clams and cockles can all be found in sand or mud. A few minutes' work with a shovel at low tide should provide the succulent main course for a meal.

Giant Pacific scallops up to 9 inches in size are found in Dixon Entrance near Rose Point, usually at depths greater than 10 fathoms. Purple-hinged rock scallops up to 10 inches in size may be found on many of the islands' rocks from low tide level to 25 fathoms. At low tide you will probably be able to find and pry the pinto abalone off the rocks — or you can scuba dive for them at any time. It's hard to beat a meal of scallops or abalone sliced thin and fried golden brown in butter.

Oysters have been introduced to the islands. They grow to maturity but do not reproduce, so be content with clams.

Check with the local fisheries representative, or phone the British Columbia red-tide hotline (604) 666-3169, before digging clams or picking

Sam Simpson, a pioneer island resident and expert razor clam digger, drops one of the delectable mollusks onto the sand of North Beach, Graham Island, a choice area for clam digging. Tow Hill, a distinctive landmark, looms in the background.

mussels. Your area may be closed because of a "saxitoxin fifty times more toxic than strychnine or curare," says marine biologist Darlene Madenwald in *Shellfish Roulette, The Red Tide Game*. This saxitoxin causes paralytic shellfish poisoning (PSP). Do not depend upon seeing the red tide; the shellfish may be toxic before there's any visual alert. Butter clams, the most abundant and widely used species, are most likely to be toxic. Razor clams are seldom affected. Twice we have seen "blooming" *Gonyaulax dinoflagellates* so dense they made patches of the sea look like tomato soup.

CHARTERING, GUIDES AND REGULATIONS

A few boats are available for charter cruises in and around the Charlottes at daily, weekly or monthly rates. Some of these boats may be skippered by longtime island residents and are often used for fishing or exclusive charters from mid-July to mid-October.

Chartering is a pleasant way to expand one's knowledge of the islands while gleaning tidbits of local lore from the skipper or just enjoying the unsurpassed coastal scenery and fishing. (See TRANSPORTATION, BOAT CHARTERS and AIR CHARTERS in the Recreational Directory.)

Guides are not required for fishing or for hunting small game, game birds or waterfowl, but many visitors choose to use a guide or go with a friend who knows the territory. That person's knowledge may make the difference between a memorable trip with a varied bag of game or fish, and a trip that was only a pleasant outdoor excursion.

Nonresidents of British Columbia hunting big game — deer, bear and elk — must be accompanied by a licensed B.C. guide. (See FISHING & HUNTING, LICENSED GUIDES in the Recreational Directory.)

Fees and regulations for hunting and fishing are subject to annual review and change. For current information write: Fish and Wildlife Branch, Ministry of the Environment and Parks, Parliament Buildings, Victoria, B.C. V8V 1X5, Canada. Information is also available from the store in each settlement where hunting and fishing licenses are sold and from the government agent or conservation agent in Queen Charlotte City.

Commencing April 1, 1981, sports fishermen require a *personal* fishing license in B.C. tidal waters for all fin fish (fish other than shellfish and crustaceans). A license is required for fishing in fresh water, as well as the special steelhead license. (See FISHING & HUNTING in the Recreational Directory.)

Aerial view of Queen Charlotte City, on the southern shore of Graham Island. Log dump and booming grounds are in the foreground; beyond is the boat haven. The distant low point is Sandspit.

Graham
Island

BY CAR
QUEEN CHARLOTTE CITY TO TLELL

Near the center of the Queen Charlottes, Queen Charlotte City (Graham Island) hugs the rocky shores of Skidegate Inlet. Here, in this fishing and logging community of approximately 1,500 persons, are the islands' general hospital, provincial and federal government offices, South Moresby National Park Headquarters, churches, hotels, a motel, bank, credit union, vehicle rental agencies, garages and service stations, a heavy equipment repair shop, post office, laundry, liquor store, RCMP station, a good boat haven, and grocery, hardware, clothing, jewelry, variety and gift stores, book sales and publication, electronics sales and repair, scuba shop, and boat sales and repair. Service clubs are the Lions International, Canadian Legion, Rod & Gun Club and Alcoholics Anonymous.

Over coffee or a meal at one of the cafes you will meet some of the island residents and discover the pervading *manana* attitude. Isolation is one of the reasons for this. Residents used to have to wait at least two weeks, and often over a month, for supplies or replacement parts to be shipped in from the mainland. Those who couldn't wait, or adapt, departed. While daily flights and frequent ferry service have reduced the transportation problem, the calm outlook has remained.

With outstanding fishing available, plus a forest full of tender venison, one is likely to forget clocks and calendars and settle in to enjoy a relaxed life. In any case, the flooding and ebbing of the tides will determine when you put your boat on the grid for bottom painting, when you dig clams, or when you hike past the white cliffs of Cape Ball.

Skidegate, also known as Skidegate Landing, is a small settlement around an open bay between Queen Charlotte City and Skidegate Mission. During the commercial fishing season a buying barge is moored to the wharf. The float serves year-round as the base for Inlet Water Taxis, a necessary service when the *Kwuna* ties up for the night after her 10:30 trip. Alongside is the all-tides ramp where the ferry *Kwuna* lands. On the opposite side is the new all-tides dock used by the *Queen of Prince Rupert* or *Queen of the North*, ferry terminal buildings and parking area. Marine fuels and fresh water are available at the adjacent pier. (See SHOPS & SERVICES, MARINE FUELS in the Recreational Directory.)

In 1976 the Queen Charlotte Islands Regional Museum was opened by

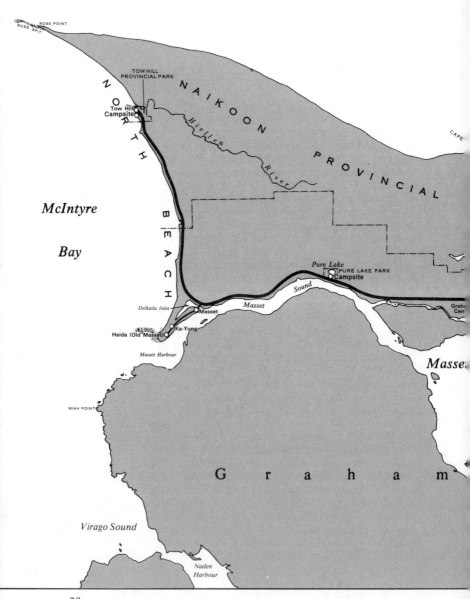

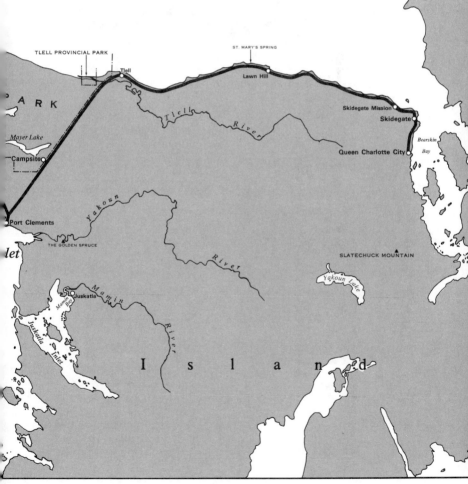

S t r a i t

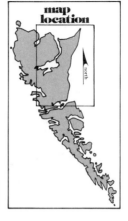

map location

north

Scale

| Kilometers | 0 | | | | 5 | | 10 | | 20 |
| Miles | 0 | | | | 5 | | 10 | |

TLELL PROVINCIAL PARK

ST. MARY'S SPRING

Tlell

Lawn Hill

P A R K

Mayer Lake

Campsite

Tlell   River

Skidegate Mission

Skidegate

Queen Charlotte City

Bearskin Bay

let

Yakoun

Port Clements

THE GOLDEN SPRUCE

River

SLATECHUCK MOUNTAIN

Yakoun Lake

Mamin

Juskatla

River

Juskatla Inlet

Mamin Bay

I   s   l   a   n   d

Above — *The Haida village
of Skidegate in 1878.*
(Provincial Archives, Victoria, B.C.)
Left — *This totem pole was
the last of many that once
stood at Skidegate. The
bottom figure is a beaver with
a gnawing stick in its paws. A
fall storm toppled the old pole
in 1987.*

Prime Minister Trudeau. The structure, located at Second Beach on the west edge of the Haida Reserve at Skidegate Mission, is architecturally harmonious with its woodside and waterfront setting. Renovated and enlarged in 1988, its attractive exhibits include: Haida totem poles, artifacts, a superb collection of argillite carvings, wooden utensils and clothing; household, school and farm equipment used by early Caucasian settlers; natural history displays, whale skulls, fossils and photographs.

Nearby are Haida longhouse-style buildings sheltering totem poles and a workshop where new totems are carved. One structure covers *Loo Taas*, the 50-foot Haida dugout canoe seen at EXPO 86. In June and July, 1987, accompanied by powered escorts, the dugout was paddled back from Vancouver to the Charlottes and beached at Skidegate Mission, to the acclaim of hundreds gathered for a modern potlatch.

More than 350 Haida Indians live in the reservation village of Skidegate Mission, a mixture of attractive frame homes, weathered buildings, a new church and a store. A single totem survives as a fitting symbol of the few Haidas and totems that now remain in the Charlottes. An attractive new office building for the local band of Haidas, constructed in the traditional style of the old longhouses, has been built on the waterfront and is enhanced by a tall dogfish totem carved by noted artist Bill Reid, assisted by other Haida artists.

Annually, on the first Saturday in June, the Haidas of Skidegate Mission celebrate the raising of this longhouse with displays of traditional Indian dancing, dress, carving, and other performances and, of course, a superb feast.

Here and in Haida (formerly called Old Masset), skilled goldsmiths and silversmiths create rings, bracelets, brooches, earrings and spoons of stylized design. Other equally talented artists choose to work with argillite, a soft, black slate found only in nearby Slatechuck Mountain and reserved for the exclusive use of the Haidas. This was probably first quarried and worked about 1820, first for curios and household uses, now for esthetic cultural expression. Still other artists fashion Haida hats and baskets of bark and roots or make silk screen designs and prints suitable for hanging. All examples of Haida artwork are much prized by residents, visitors and museums. The works of Victor Adams, Gordon Cross, Claude Davidson, Robert Davidson, Rufus Moody, Bill Reid and other Haidas have won international recognition. (See SHOPS & SERVICES.)

Shortly before 1900 the few survivors of the dying Haida villages reluctantly abandoned their isolated ancestral homes and moved into Skidegate Mission or Old Masset. The problem of too many chiefs and not enough villages was resolved by acknowledging the supremacy of the chief of Skidegate Mission and the chief of Old Masset, and recognizing the responsibility of the newly arrived chiefs for their own bands. This was the nadir of the culture of the artistic, sea-oriented Haidas who only 100 years earlier had been estimated to number in excess of 8,000, living in at least 17 villages. By 1915 there were only 588 Haidas. Now there are about 1,300 living in the Charlottes.

For those planning to visit any of the abandoned Haida villages south of Graham Island, call in at the Skidegate Band Council in Skidegate Mission (phone 559-4496) to purchase permits: $25 per person, per year. Permits to visit Ninstints on Anthony Island Provincial Park are obtained there at no charge.

To see the old village sites on Graham and Langara islands, apply at the Haida Council in Haida (phone 626-3925). Permits for all Masset Band reserves are $15 per person.

If you do not have your own boat, you may decide to charter a boat, helicopter or amphibious plane. Considering all factors, you may conclude that it is economical to charter a four-passenger helicopter at about $575 per hour of flight time. By paying for 2½ to 3½ hours you may, depending upon time of year, have the helo all day — plenty of time for sightseeing,

The bow section of the 2,150-ton Pesuta, *wrecked by a December storm in 1928 just north of the mouth of the Tlell River. This can be reached by a pleasant and scenic hike commencing at the Tlell River bridge, southern entrance to Naikoon Provincial Park.*

photographing, beachcombing or exploring mountain meadows alive with tiny flowers, or lonely beaches that catch drift from far-off places. The popular Bell Jet Rangers cruise at 110 miles (180 km) per hour. If your party is fewer than four, the helicopter base manager may know of others who will fill the helo and share the cost. (See TRANSPORTATION, AIR CHARTERS, BOAT CHARTERS & WATER TAXIS.)

The flat east side of Graham Island is the land of the homesteaders. Old trails and overgrown clearings mark disheartening failures. Now, an ever-increasing number of comfortable new homes rim shore and roadside. New dirt roads or trails often lead through the second-growth forest to owner-built homes of attractive design.

A scenic 2-lane asphalt road curves up the coast along the drift-covered shores of Hecate Strait, through open range country where plodding Herefords or shaggy Scottish highland cattle graze. Near Lawn Hill and on the road's seaward side, a number of tall stumps have been transformed into life-size birds and animals by the skilled chain-saw sculpture of Ted Bellis, a local resident.

North of Lawn Hill is St. Mary's Spring, often a welcome stop for the thirsty traveler. Local legend has it that whoever drinks of this cool water will someday return to the islands. A Madonna, carved by Mr. Bellis, decorates this turnout.

Eight miles south of the Tlell River Bridge, on the seaward side of the highway, is Davis Road leading to the Bottle and Jug Works, where attractive hand-crafted pottery is created and sold.

Just 35 kilometers (22 miles) north of Skidegate Mission, the scattered ranching community of Tlell nestles between a windbreak of low tree-covered dunes and the serpentine Tlell River. An animal hospital and boarding and grooming facilities are available at the scenic Richardson Ranch. This area is a fisherman's delight, for only a few steps from the homestead are deep pools where salmon, trout or steelhead lurk.

Headquarters of the Naikoon Provincial Park are alongside the highway at the Dunes, just south of the Tlell River bridge. The park, established in 1973, (72,640 hectares or 179,500 acres) encompasses most of northeastern Graham Island.

The park supervisor is glad to answer questions about the park, established trails, campgrounds and picnic sites, and tell you whether you are likely to see whistling swans, sandhill cranes or Canada geese along the Tlell River lowlands. He may even share information about the better fishing spots and recommend lures or flies.

Just north of headquarters is Misty Meadows, a pleasant campground with 30 campsites and a picnic area nestling among the windblown trees. Here, and in other provincial campgrounds, a small fee may be collected during the summer. On the northwest side of the river is a parking and picnic site. A popular hike begins here, goes through the dim rain forest and along the Tlell River to its mouth, then strikes out across a storm-tumbled gravel beach where an occasional agate sparkles.

Then onward to the weathered bow of an old wooden vessel, the *Pesuta*, wrecked during a southeast storm in December 1928. She was a 264-foot log barge under tow when she struck bottom and the towline parted. Wind and seas drove her hard aground. The tug escaped and no one was lost.

This is a pleasant jaunt of about 10 kms (6 miles), round-trip. It could also be the start of a hike up the coast, fording small, dark streams, passing a couple of cabins, using the hand-ferry across the Ball River, and coming out on the road to Tow Hill. It is a 55-mile hike if you use the Cape Fife Trail, longer if you round Rose Spit. Hiking from south to north is easier and more pleasant, as the prevailing wind will push you along.

The Golden Spruce.

Water along the low area is brown and should be boiled for drinking. There is no water between Cape Fife and Tow Hill.

Primitive camping is permitted throughout the park.

Argonaut Hill, flat-topped and wooded to its summit, near the northeast tip of Graham Island, is one of the park's most prominent topographical features. It rises from the Argonaut Plain to some 150 meters (492 feet) above sea level.

TLELL TO HAIDA

After crossing the Tlell River the road turns inland, running straight across about 19 kilometers (12 miles) of lowlands. Here you'll see spongy marshland where blackened snags tell of an old forest fire. Midway along this road on the right side is the 1-kilometer-long gravel road to picnic tables, firepits and toilets on the sandy shores of Mayer Lake, where one may swim, fish or launch small boats. In mid-July, 19 common loons serenaded us with their haunting, yodel-like laughs as they swam and dived near the yellow water lilies on the lake's rim. From here the road goes to Port Clements, an early settlement on Masset Inlet that is now a logging and fishing community of about 500 people. The community has a small-boat haven and a wharf where marine fuels may be obtained. General stores, cafes, a motel, service station, post office, rock shop, sporting goods store, and churches complete the community center. Service clubs are Lions International and Rod & Gun Club. About 1.5 kilometers northeast of town is the abandoned settlement of Graham Centre. For those traveling in RVs or campers, a sani-station and fresh water supply are maintained.

Port Clements is best known for its proximity to the Golden Spruce, a 165 foot tall tree more than 300 years old, with gold-covered needles. In recent years other "golden" spruce have been discovered on the Charlottes, but this particular spruce on the west bank of the Yakoun River is the largest and most famous.

To see the Golden Spruce, head southwest out of Port Clements for about 5.5 kilometers (3.5 miles) to a small turnout on your right where a sign marks the start of a short trail winding among giant trees to the Yakoun River. On the opposite shore stands the healthy Golden Spruce, in sharp contrast to a background of ordinary trees.

After returning to your car, continue toward Juskatla for another 8 kilometers (5 miles) until finding a spur road on your left marked by the silhouette of a canoe. This goes through a clearcut area to a well-marked trail leading to a shaped but uncompleted dugout canoe nearly 50 feet in length. Nearby lies a great western red cedar that was cut, chiseled and probed to its heart by Haida canoe carvers. The carvers were testing the soundness of the tree which from the exterior appeared suitable for canoe building, but wasn't.

Gold was discovered in the vicinity of Juskatla-Port Clements more than a decade ago. A pilot crushing mill was brought in and operated, then removed. City Resources (Canada) Ltd. has completed the first phases of the Cinola Gold Project, covering a broad spectrum of public concerns including environmental studies, pollution control and job opportunties. The gold is there and the price is right, but diverse groups oppose this industry.

Returning to Port Clements you resume driving north over smooth roads through country that is rolling and forested. Nearly halfway along this 45-kilometer (28 mile) trip to Masset is Pure Lake Park, a pleasant rest area where picnic tables, firepits and toilet facilities have been erected along the shores of placid Pure Lake. Diminutive coniferous trees and low salal bushes add beauty and privacy to the area.

Masset is the Charlottes' largest settlement. A majority of its 2,000 residents are employed in some facet of the fishing industry or at the Canadian Armed Forces Station. A canning and freezing plant along the east side of Masset Sound is the scene of great activity during the fishing season as fishermen hurry to unload their catches, take on loads of chipped ice and fuel, then rush back to the fishing grounds.

Here are cafes, inn, hotel; grocery, hardware, clothing, variety and gift stores; credit union; churches, physicians, dentist, public health nurse offices; fuel supplies, garages and service stations, vehicle rental agencies; post office, RCMP station, liquor store, golf course; public sani-station and a private recreational park with hook-ups. Emergency and evening pharmacy services are available at the Canadian Forces Station Hospital. The Jessie Simpson Library is an attractive example of peeled-log construction and well worth seeing inside as well as out. Service clubs are Canadian Legion, Lions International, Rod & Gun Club and Alcoholics Anonymous.

Work began in late 1987 on a municipal airport east of Masset. The land has been cleared and graveling is scheduled for completion in May, 1989.

Tiny Delkatla Inlet probes into town and is a fine boat haven filled with sport boats and the local fishing fleet. Scheduled and charter flights of amphibious planes operated by Trans-Provincial Airlines and North Coast Air Services operate from here. (See TRANSPORTATION, AIR in the Recreational Directory.)

A variety of waterfowl can be observed in Delkatla Wildlife Sanctuary, at the head of Delkatla Inlet. The largest birds usually seen there are the rust-colored sandhill cranes, which stop during spring and fall migrations. Whistling swans often winter in the Charlottes but frequently seek more scheduled waterways.

About 3 kilometers (2 miles) north, along the shore of Masset Harbour, some 650 Haidas live in the reservation village of Haida. Here, various styles of Haida art in several media are for sale, and the artist may be available to explain the significance of your selection. Nearby is the abandoned Indian village of Ka-Yung, where for many years stood the only totem pole in the area. However, in 1969, a talented young artist, Robert Davidson, completed a tall totem honoring his grandfather, Chief Gungyah. At a large gathering of local, mainland and Alaskan Haidas, many of them clad in traditional costumes, the handsome pole was erected to the accompaniment of traditional singing and dancing. By 1975 more new poles were added to the village's grassy recreation field, just below the Ed Jones Haida Museum.

Shiny agates or red carnelian pebbles can be found on the gravel beach beyond the village. Sometimes saucer-size scallop shells, sand dollars or glass fishing floats from Japan may also be found.

MASSET TO NAIKOON PROVINCIAL PARK

One should make the 26-km (16-mile) drive along the north coast from Masset, past the Dixon Entrance Golf Course and the Canadian Forces Station to Tow Hill. The first half is asphalt; the rest is narrow, of hard-packed sand or gravel, and wends through trees bearded with lichens and heavy with moss, past pleasing new homes. Signs indicating access to the long sand beach read, "Four-wheel drive recommended."

Part of this area, where Spanish moss hangs like dainty lacework from the widespread branches of ancient spruce trees, is the Tow Hill Ecological Reserve. There is another reserve at Rose Spit.

With Tow Hill looming ahead, you come to Agate Beach Campground, 20 units, an attractive, well-maintained camp and picnic area overlooking the active waters of Dixon Entrance. Nearby are a fresh-water pump, firewood and toilets.

At Tow Hill Picnic Grounds, tables and fire pits nestle under great spruce and cedar trees along the Hiellen River. A trail winds along the shore, up and along the top of a 400-foot perpendicular cliff of columnar basalt (a good place for photos), and to the top of 500-foot Tow Hill, then twists

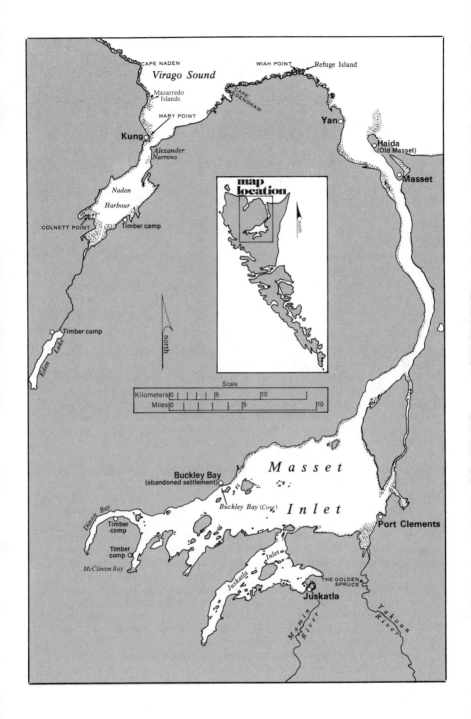

down to the picnic area.

The road ends at the beach on the east side of the Hiellen River. Though the sand is hard, it is easy to sink a two-wheel-drive vehicle up to its axles—and the tide seems to rush in aggressively at such times.

From the hill, on a clear day, one may gaze beyond the restless waters of Dixon Entrance, across the Canadian/U.S. border, to the snow-painted mountains of Dall and Prince of Wales islands in Alaska. To the west, past the steel-blue waters of McIntyre Bay and low Wiah Point, lies the dark form of Langara Island. Some McIntyre Bay beaches are nearly 300 meters (330 yards) wide, and usually they are separated from the tree-covered dunes by stormtossed drift logs. To the east you see the golden sands of North Beach inviting you to hike the eight miles to Rose Point. The Haidas call it Naikoon, meaning "long nose."

Beyond is Rose Spit, an extensive finger of tidal sand where Dixon Entrance and Hecate Strait meet in jumbled torment. You may see crabbers pulling in pots of Dungeness crabs or, at low tide, people scurrying along the wave-lapped shore, digging the elusive razor clams.

Near Tow Hill is the Blow Hole, a natural channel in the basalt where, when tide and waves cooperate, salt water shoots upward with impressive sound and force.

The Cape Fife Trail starts east of Tow Hill and crosses the Argonaut Plain — an area of meadows, muskeg, meandering streams, stunted and wind-deformed pines and low, flat-topped hills — to Fife Point on Hecate Strait, a hike of 10 kms. A longer trail follows the Hiellen River inland to Clearwater Lake, and on to Hecate Strait.

Driving on the beach is recommended only in four-wheel-drive vehicles. Maps posted at access roads and campgrounds show the permitted routes within Naikoon Park. All are below the drift line except for the route through the Rose Spit Ecological Reserve. For safety, two or more vehicles should travel together and carry such emergency equipment as winches and shovels, and, of course, tide charts.

You are now ready to enjoy a trip to Rose Point, across the curving beach where hard-packed sand slopes up to a bulwark of silver drift logs. Continue to Rose Spit, where winter storms have tossed logs onto grass-covered dunes. You may find a Japanese glass net float or storm-dredged scallop shells. Gulls, ravens and sandpipers will be your companions.

Inveterate hikers or backpackers may want to turn south, down the east coast, along miles of sand hills covered with coarse vegetation. Wild cattle, descendents of stock introduced by the pioneers, once roamed this desolate area where cliffs of sand and clay attain heights of 400 feet. The woods are interspersed with patches of swampland draining into small dark-colored streams, some stagnant or brackish. Pack that container of fresh water, and don't get trapped against sheer cliffs by a flooding tide and pounding surf. The stark, weathered timbers of the 2,154-ton *Pesuta* signal that your hike is nearly completed; only 5 kilometers (3 miles) to the Tlell River bridge where, usually, a hiker can get a ride into town. Hikers may expect to find more sea shells — especially saucer-size weathervane scallops — and more glass balls than it will be practical to carry on the 74-kilometer (46 mile) trip.

Indians in Haida and in Skidegate Mission use traditional designs in figures made of argillite, a soft black slate found only in nearby Slatechuck Mountain and reserved for the exclusive use of the Haidas. (BRITISH COLUMBIA GOVERNMENT)

PORT CLEMENTS TO QUEEN CHARLOTTE CITY

If you are in Port Clements on a weekend or one of those long summer evenings (it's often light until after 10:30) and prefer to see some new and different country as you return to Queen Charlotte City, head out of town on the road taken to see the Golden Spruce. Ahead, only 19 kilometers (12 miles) from "Port," is Juskatla, local headquarters of MacMillan Bloedel Industries, located on Mamin Bay in Juskatla Inlet.

In addition to seeing the log dump and sorting grounds, stop at the office to learn if the roads are clear of trucks and to pick up a free road map. This map shows the main road from Port Clements to Queen Charlotte

City, plus hundreds of miles of side roads, campsites, picnic areas, boat launches, viewpoints and places of interest. You may be intrigued by some of the names: Ghost, Phantom, Canoe, Hoodoo, Blackbear, Blackwater and Gold creeks. Sections of these roads are open to unrestricted travel; other sections are in use during working hours.

You will see some magnificent scenery, and drive along enticing streams where salmon, trout or steelheads await the fisherman. The Yakoun River

Commercial salmon trollers moored to floats at Wiah Point on the north coast of Graham Island. This is a good place to wait out a storm or glean information from the fishermen.

is one of the Charlottes' great steelhead streams. Chinook and coho salmon also spawn here. Haidas of the Masset Band are enhancing the Yakoun's chinook run with their hatchery at Marie Lake.

You can obtain this map at MacMillan Bloedels' shop near the west end of Queen Charlotte City. (Or, write MacMillan Bloedel Industries Ltd., Box 10, Juskatla, B.C. V0T 1J0, asking for their recreational guide to the Queen Charlotte Division.)

Make sure your gas tank is full and the spare tire is inflated. If the roads are clear, backtrack a few kilometers until you cross the high bridge over the Mamin River, then turn south onto the main logging road meandering through the broad valley of the Yakoun River and into the heartland of Graham Island.

Sparkling streams pour into lakes that are fringed with water lilies and nearly hidden in vast tracts of virgin timber. The road threads in and out between logged-off slopes, and spur roads snake up hillsides to gouged earth and piles of broken timber, the scars and debris of loading operations. These clearcut areas when reseeded by nature or replanted quickly become cover and feed for birds as well as for deer and bear. In 60 to 80 years a new crop of trees will be ready for harvesting.

A raven flying directly from Juskatla to Queen Charlotte City would travel less than 40 kilometers (25 miles). But the scenic drive, rolling down the foothills of Slatechuck Mountain to Bearskin Bay and then into "Charlotte," covers nearly 64 kilometers (40 miles).

BY BOAT
MASSET INLET TO LEPAS BAY

Sailors arriving in the Charlottes in rough weather may want to quiet queasy stomachs by spending a few days cruising the smooth tree-fringed waters of Masset and Juskatla inlets. (Before entering any area where the flow of salt water may be restricted, check your *Sailing Directions, British Columbia Coast [North Portion],*because the various tidal streams can attain velocities up to nine knots.) Watch as massive barges with two or three towering cranes load over two million board feet of prime logs in less than 24 hours. Poke around the 65-year-old ruins on Buckley Bay (Cove). This was once a sawmill settlement where 400 men were employed and was also a freight and passenger stop for the old SS *Prince John.* Cross to a nearby island and search along the beach for fossilized wood, or at

Pillar Rock, a 95-foot column of conglomerate rock and sandstone is a conspicuous landmark on the north coast of Graham Island.

high tide take a lightweight skiff up the Yakoun River and see the Golden Spruce. Be prepared to drag the skiff across a snag or two.

Incidentally, all mariners in and around the Charlottes should keep a sharp lookout for drifting logs and deadheads — water-soaked logs that have little buoyancy and often float vertically, sometimes disappear below the surface for a few seconds, then drive upward, breaking the surface and projecting two or three feet into the air — or through a hull. Some deadheads rest on end on the bottom, their tops angled just below the surface, ready to joust with any unwary boater.

Beginning at Masset and cruising west, visit and photograph the abandoned Indian village of Yan, across the harbor from Haida, where a few deteriorating totems hide amidst lush greenery. The Yan Eagle once stood here, one of the most beautiful of totems, with a sparkling abalone-shell breast, a sharp curved beak and graceful feathers. Gray, cracked cedar totems, splotchy with moss and lichens, now merely hint of Yan's former splendor.

A courtesy call on the Chief of Haida, or at the tribal band office, requesting permission to visit Yan, is in order. It is also an excellent excuse to meet one or more of the dignified, mellow-voiced Haidas. If you do not have a small boat, the chief may know where one can be hired.

Fishermen talk of Seven Mile but charts show the name Wiah Point. Whatever, scores of trollers and gillnetters charge through the narrow passage between Wiah Point and Refuge Island, which is marked by a light

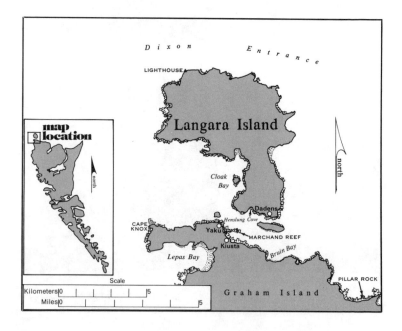

buoy and a light, and moor to a float for a short night's rest. See this evening ritual. You might want to talk with some of these self-reliant men who know intimately the waters from Vancouver to Prince Rupert. But tie up next to the float, not outboard of a nest of trollers, for these boats will be under way before dawn to catch the morning bite.

Heading westward along a low nearly featureless coast past Cape Edenshaw, you find Virago Sound funneling you in toward Mary Point and the abandoned Haida village of Kung, on the sandy beaches of Alexander Narrows. This is the entrance to Naden Harbour, for 30 years home port for a fleet of whalers that kept over 100 Japanese laborers busy flensing and processing massive carcasses into thousands of barrels of oil — and surrounding the station with a scum of slippery, malodorous waste. Now derelict brick fireboxes and a tall square concrete tower stand on the western shore beside a beach speckled with clinkers and fragments of whalebone. Fallen wooden structures and boards with rusted nails are scattered over a few acres of once cleared land. Opposite, on the eastern shore, are a logging camp and a sportsfishing lodge.

Naden Harbour is a good place to try out your crab or prawn trap. Bait it with an old fish head or a punctured can of sardines.

A steel-hulled log barge has been sunk near Colnett Point, at the head of Naden Harbour, as a breakwater for the booming grounds. A logging road extends south through a broad valley to a modern trailer camp for employees of a lumber company on the shore of Eden Lake. This is Canada's westernmost logging operation.

Mooring buoys have been placed on the southern side of the Mazarredo Islands, on the western side of Virago Sound.

Nineteen kilometers (12 miles) west of Cape Naden is Pillar Rock, rising 95 feet above a tidal ledge. This unique and picturesque column of conglomerate rock and sandstone is covered with a headdress of brush and trees. A pair of Peale's peregrine falcons has nested on this sheer rock safe from enemies, overlooking an ample supply of sea-bird prey. This distinctive falcon is seen and heard along the Charlottes' lonely coasts. Mooring buoys are located in Pillar Bay.

West of the anchorage in Bruin Bay (mooring buoys) is an opening on the southeast side of Marchand Reef, affording access to a gravel beach in front of sad-faced totems at the twin abandoned Haida villages of Kiusta and Yaku. Children once played in the grassy clearing where deer now browse and human bones are sometimes scuffed up. Mooring buoys are in front of Kiusta.

After an encouraging exploratory dig at Kiusta in 1972, archaeologists returned in 1973 with a crew of two dozen young assistants and began excavating. A number of Indian artifacts were discovered, identified and catalogued during the winter. Further excavations have been made since then. Weathered totem poles, an old cannon and most of the artifacts found at Kiusta are on display in the Ed Jones Haida museum in Haida.

A well-blazed mile-long trail follows the valley floor between Kiusta and crescent-shaped Lepas Bay. The sandy beach of the bay, on the west side of the island, is a good place to search for Japanese glass balls tossed ashore by waves breaking on the bay's shallow bottom and rolling across

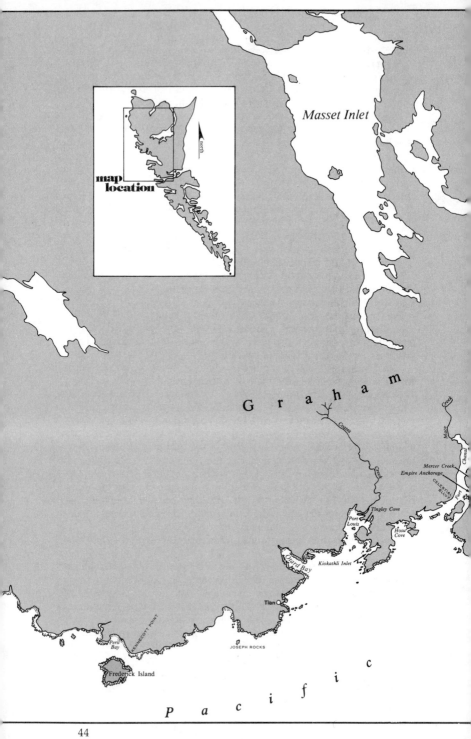

Masset Inlet

G r a h a m

Coates

Creek

Creek

Mace

Port

Chanal

Merver Creek.
Empire Anchorage
CELESTIAL
BLUFF

Tingley Cove

Port
Louis

*Hosu'
Cove*

Otard Bay

Kiokathli Inlet

Tian

*Peril
Bay*

KENNECOTT POINT

JOSEPH ROCKS

Frederick Island

P   a   c   i   f   i   c

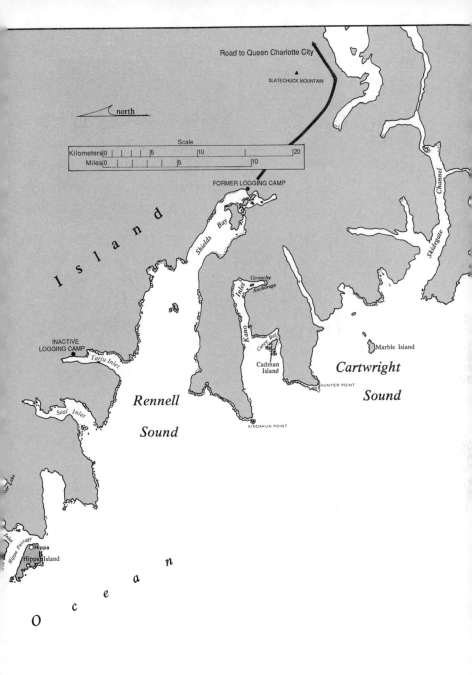

Road to Queen Charlotte City

SLATECHUCK MOUNTAIN

north

Scale

Kilometers 0 | | | | 5 | 10 | 20

Miles 0 | | | | 5 | 10

FORMER LOGGING CAMP

I s l a n d

Shields Bay

Givenchy
Anchorage

Kano Inlet

Carew Bay

INACTIVE
LOGGING CAMP

Tartu Inlet

Cadman
Island

Marble Island

Cartwright

HUNTER POINT

Sound

Rennell

Sound

Seal Inlet

KINDAKUN POINT

Skidegate Channel

r Lake

Inlet

Hippa Passage

Hippa
Hippa Island

O c e a n

O

Sea-sculptured limestone is exposed at low tide near Kennecott Point. Trees killed by gales form a backdrop along this stony beach where agates sparkle and glass balls from Japanese fishing gear float ashore. Nearby Peril Bay is frequently filled with commercial fishing vessels on summer nights.

the sandy beach toward you. This is also a good spot to begin a hike of a few days southward along the relatively low, often sandy shores to Peril Bay.

LANGARA ISLAND

Rare peregrine falcons and their prey, auklets and murrelets, nest on the rocky and precipitous coast of wooded Langara Island. Other birds abounding in this remote area are bald eagles, belted kingfishers, pigeon guillemots, murres, glaucous-winged gulls, surf birds, black turnstones, black oystercatchers, mergansers, loons and a wide assortment of surface-feeding and bay ducks.

Circumnavigation of the island is worthwhile, especially if it includes a visit with the lightkeepers. (Some Canadian lights are maintained by small civilian staffs, often a family or two. We have always found the keepers hospitable, eager to talk with visitors and most interesting.) However, the landing is difficult, and a skipper might choose to stay with his boat.

You can moor to one of the three buoys in Beal Cove on the west side of the abandoned Haida village of Dadens, moor to buoys in Cloak Bay, or anchor in nearby Henslung Cove. Fishermen here are a ready source of information concerning sea conditions to the westward, though they may toss in a few barbed remarks about the sanity of anyone who would choose to spend a holiday on that wide open, uninhabited changeable coast.

In season, a sports-fishing lodge on a barge is moored in Henslung Cove, an excellent area to fish for large coho or chinook salmon.

LANGARA ISLAND TO TIAN

Black reefs of eroded volcanic rock alternate with smooth sandy beaches along Graham Island's wild west coast. On many of these open, agate-speckled beaches landing is seldom feasible, but when seas are calm rewards for the beachcomber are great. Among the treasures found here have been long bamboo poles up to 6 inches in diameter, notched and fitted with line for use on Oriental craft; tall, tapered saki bottles; glass fishing floats, some larger than basketballs, a few wrapped in colorful net; life rings

Hosu Cove, Graham Island. Neil and Betty Carey beachcombing and storm watching during a northwest gale. (Dr. Peter Mylechreest)

painted with names of distant ports; wooden kegs bound with strips of bamboo and redolent of soy or pickled daikon; 5-gallon-size Oriental crockery jugs of the type used to age sweet rice wine; plastic or tin containers with Japanese or Russian pictures and writing on them.

Occasionally a dead whale, orca or shark washes ashore. Most die of natural causes; some, after encounters with ships or killer whales. After bears and eagles have cleaned the bones, they come apart and are scattered by storm waves. They endure for years, and may be found on any shore. The white teeth of the sperm whale, often banana-size, are prize finds.

47

The carcass of a killer whale, complete with skull and teeth, was found in Kaisun Harbour in 1987.

With sharp eyes, great luck and miles of hiking lonely shores, you may find some of these treasures, even shark teeth. We are happy if we pick up one whale tooth every two or three years. One summer, on a rugged west-coast beach where I'd once found a sperm tooth, I found a harpoon. Its nose cone had exploded and its four barbs were rusted open. It was brutally heavy, but I did not leave it behind. Fury Bay's gravel beach may yield a few more sperm teeth to a diligent beachcomber.

The varied and fiercely beautiful, but often inhospitable, shores between Henslung Cove on Langara Island and Port Louis on Graham Island are the longest stretch on the Charlottes' west coast unbroken by any sheltering inlet. Lepas, Sialun, and Beresford bays are enticing, but row after row of building, cresting, and breaking waves charging up wide beaches of golden sand make landings difficult and launchings nearly impossible most of the time. Hiking or helicoptering in are the safest methods.

Port Chanal, Graham Island, looking from between Goose Cove and Empire Anchorage toward Celestial Bluff. Port Chanal is a quiet moorage or anchorage where rockhounds search for petrified wood, fishermen jig for halibut or cast for salmon, and anyone enjoys the beauty of the area where birds and animals abound. There are many such spots along Graham Island's west coast.

The rolling waters off Frederick Island — which has mooring buoys on the northeast side — offer indifferent protection for the sailor resting overnight or waiting out a storm. Eastward of the island is aptly named Peril Bay, which has a golden beach that curves to Kennecott Point. South of the point a loose gravel beach, pinched between a wide flat reef and upswept banks, glitters with agates, some larger than baseballs. Jet-black fossilized wood from prehistoric trees is often uncovered by churning seas.

A colony of nearly 400 sea lions hauls out on sea-washed Joseph Rocks. Approaching slowly, a visitor can get within camera range while great bulls weighing up to a ton each belch and order the much smaller females off to investigate the newcomer. When you get within a few yards, the rocks become a mass of slithering brown bodies caroming pellmell into the sea as the females seek refuge from the human visitor. Finally, with obvious reluctance, the truculent bulls gracefully arc into the foaming waters. Slim heads pop out of the water and the sea lions roar until the intruder leaves. Then, surf riding with superb agility, the animals return to their slippery rock and interrupted rest.

Of the approximately 5,000 sea lions along the British Columbia coast, over half find shelter and food, mostly scrap fish, in waters around the Queen Charlottes. In midsummer of 1974 scientists from the University of British Columbia tagged 263 sea lion pups born on rocks off Cape St. James, at the southern tip of the Charlottes. *It is illegal — and senseless — to shoot any marine mammals.*

Weary totems, many split by trees and shrubs rooted inside them, lean among trees near rectangular excavations where great longhouses once stood on knolls at the abandoned Indian village of Tian. Even today it is easy to see why the ancient Haidas loved this sunny village, built near salmon streams and only minutes away by dugout canoe from banks teeming with lingcod and halibut, well protected from raiding parties by many miles of open sea. Lying in the village are tangled wire rope, stacks of drill rods and a small steam engine, flaky with rust, near a six-inch pipe burbling brackish, sulfurous water — the futile end of a pre-World War I search for oil.

PORT LOUIS TO HIPPA ISLAND

If you are caught in a summer fog, or stormbound for a day or so (and this can happen in summer when a local gale can strike without warning, and water tumbles from the hillsides in many cascades and runnels), Port Louis, Port Chanal or Nesto Inlet are snug places to be anchored or moored. There is always plenty to do in any of these areas for crew members of any age. In fine weather it is too easy to hoist the anchor and promise yourself a better look next time.

Tingley Cove in Port Louis is a secure anchorage. From here you may hike the kilometer-long gravel road leading west from an abandoned loading pier to a cleared and leveled area of about an acre where, in 1971, the Union Oil Company drilled to 5,000 feet. Or at high tide, run the outboard up to the chattering falls of Coates Creek, fishing along the way. Hunt or photograph deer along the grassy flats. Walk kilometers of varied shores, beachcombing or rock hounding. Comfortable cabins stand within the shelter of Port Louis. Agates and red jasper, surf-tumbled and smooth, abound on a sequestered beach northeast of Louis Point.

It's only a short hike from Kiokathli Inlet (mooring buoys) across grassy, sparsely treed lowlands to wildly magnificent Hosu Cove. During a westerly storm this rock- and reef-cluttered cove is frosted with scudding foam tossed from rampaging breakers.

If you're lucky and catch the sea reasonably quiet, Hosu Cove is worth

Betty Carey stands by the bow section of the USATS Clarksdale Victory, *wrecked on Hippa Island during a stormy night in November 1947 with the loss of 49 lives.*

hours of exploration by boat and afoot. Though not properly surveyed, and encumbered by islets and underwater obstructions, you may, with care, "read" the water and enjoy Hosu's many tiny bays with beaches of sand, gravel, or boulders — sheltered between headlands of rough, angular rock, or hidden behind narrow islets — all sloping up to the windblown forest crisscrossed with game trails. A small stream empties through a long gulch at the northeast side.

The mooring buoys in Port Chanal are a good base for exploration or for fishing for halibut and lingcod. The photogenic islets and rocky point between Empire Anchorage and the buoys lie within the north border of an ecological reserve. Nearby is Mercer Creek, a short, winding stream tumbling through a valley of spruce and cedars. The creek flows from Mercer Lake, where sockeye salmon return to spawn each summer. Rock hounds should find a few pieces of fossilized wood during a hike over the stones of Mace Creek at the head of Port Chanal. Caves along the north shore, beyond Celestial Bluff, will entertain any spelunkers among the crew.

In the unnamed and incompletely surveyed bay between Selvesen and Marchand points, grotesque rock formations, arches and sheer battered cliffs rim a rocky bay, and ragged, gale-torn trees, climbing to tall snow-smothered mountains, make excellent subjects for many pictures. Even in quiet weather, the seas usually surge powerfully in and out of most narrow leads to the shore.

Nesto Inlet, entered from Hippa Passage, is good shelter, has excellent fishing and can be your base for investigating the many sandy beaches pinched between fingers of rock along the north side of the passage. Haidas once lived in this area, though no totems exist today.

We were moored here in June when a large black bear ambled out of the bush to feed on tall salt grass near the stream. Soon he walked over to a small spruce tree, stood up to his full height, grasped a limb high overhead and commenced scratching his back against the trunk, shaking the entire tree. Another time, during the salmon spawning season, four bears were fishing at the stream's mouth. One large fellow failed to snag a fish. Finally, frustrated, he leaped from a rock into the pool where many salmon congregated, spray flew in all directions as he hit with a mighty bellyflop — and still no salmon!

Pull a skiff ashore on Hippa Island and spend a day hiking. Search for the abandoned Indian village of Hippa and a World War II coast watch cabin or cross the lowland and hike the volcanic beach to visit the wrecked *Clarksdale Victory.*

High on the shelving reef on Hippa Island's south side is the bow section of what was once a U.S. Army transport ship. At low tide, one can climb aboard and walk along the canted decks that are thick with rust and littered with broken anchor chain and cargo-handling equipment. Cargo booms fitted with heavy blocks hang over the side, trailing whiskered rigging. Departing Whittier, Alaska, in November 1947, the *Clarksdale Victory* stranded and then broke in two. All but 4 of the crew of 53 perished during a gale, while U.S. Coast Guard planes and ships from Alaska fought the winds and seas — trying to reach and rescue the seamen.

RENNELL SOUND TO SKIDEGATE CHANNEL

Salmon trollers ply the waters of Rennell Sound, which is bounded by snow-peaked mountains and reaches 18 miles into Graham Island. Until 1983 a logging camp was located on the flats of Shields Bay. The company constructed a private logging road through a low mountain pass to connect with the road between Queen Charlotte City and Juskatla. On Sundays or after working hours it is possible for a fisherman or explorer to drive on that road to this west coast sound and launch a small boat.

If you don't care to go to the head of Rennell Sound for a safe anchorage, you might try rugged Seal Inlet. Though its entrance is littered with rocks, one can find shelter at the head of the inlet near the extensive grassy flats amid several interesting islets. Or go past Seal Inlet to Tartu Inlet and tie up to the mooring buoys. A truck-logging camp is located here, serviced by amphibian aircraft and helicopters.

At the turn of the century a sailing ship was wrecked on the bouldered shore between Rennell Sound and Kindakun Point. An elderly Haida chief gave us a few clues but it was not until 1973 — after extensive research — that Betty and I identified the remains of the wrecked ship as the 223-foot *Florence*. Unheard of for months after leaving Puget Sound with a load of coal for the Oahu Railroad, in Hawaii, she was at last logged "missing at sea, all hands presumed lost." In July 1973 we assisted in recovering the ship's rare Trotman anchor.

In June of 1985 we assisted eleven members of the Duncan family — great and great-great grandchildren of Capt. Fred Duncan, who was captain of the *Florence* for fourteen years, but not at the time the ship was lost — recover the second one-ton anchor of the *Florence*. Both recoveries were made after thorough planning, on long, exciting days of arduous work blessed with reasonably calm seas.

Givenchy Anchorage at the head of Kano Inlet affords good shelter, has a mooring buoy and freshwater hose, plus a view of steep mountains.

Part of your crew might enjoy lolling on one of the sand beaches — only a short swim from the mooring buoys — in Carew Bay, near the entrance to the inlet, while others are off jigging for cod near Cadman Island.

Foul ground and extensive kelp beds surround Hunter Point, where massive boulders hold a few twisted frames and plates from the MV *Kennecott*. This U.S. ship was destined for a Tacoma, Washington, smelter with 6,000 tons of high-grade copper ore from Cordova, Alaska, when fall currents and a northwest gale combined to set her east of her course and she ran hard aground one night in October 1923. Similar sea conditons in 1964 parted the thick towline of Portland-bound supply barge #539 and set it almost on top of the *Kennecott*. Large tires mounted on heavy rims, rusted oil drums and tanks for compressed gas are all that remain. No lives were lost in either disaster.

Construction began in 1987 of a Coast Guard radio site on Hunter Point. Seas offshore are often confused, especially shortly after the tide turns. Conditons improve after one rounds the long, shelving reef and swings into Cartwright Sound. Remains of a World War II radar station can be seen in a semisheltered pocket on the north side of Marble Island. Green camouflage paint splotches the siding of a gale-flattened mess hall, some barracks and workshops. Almost lost in thick brush is a funicular hoist and decayed steps leading to the weatherbeaten tower and hilltop barracks. If the weather is clear, the climb is worthwhile because of the superb view of the surrounding seascape. Landings on Marble Island are not easy, even during calm seas, because of the heavy surge.

Excellent fresh water may be obtained year-round from a hose at the buoy near the head of Dawson Harbour where, during the fishing season, commercial fishermen congregate at night.

Tidal streams of up to seven knots are created in the narrows between Graham and Moresby islands, because the tides at Queen Charlotte City, on the east, range to 26 feet on a large tide, while tides at Trounce Inlet to the west range to only 15 feet. On one's first passage it is advisable to enter on a flooding tide. Slack water occurs about three hours after high or low water at Queen Charlotte City. Check your chart and *Sailing Directions, British Columbia Coast (North Portion)*. Concentrate on piloting your boat through this narrow sluiceway while other members of the crew stay clear of the pilothouse and snap pictures of the glorious scenery, a variety of waterfowl and birds, and alert animals.

Even experienced skippers may run afoul when tidal forces are near maximum. In mid-July, 1987, from a helicopter, I photographed two fifty-foot seiners near the west end of the Narrows. One was hard aground on a gravel bar, with the tide ebbing rapidly. The other lay on her beam ends, flooded, with seine net and floats swirling around her stern. All hands were rescued and the vessels were refloated.

Near the East Narrows at low water you may see the remains of the *Cape Fox*, a seiner that ran aground during an ebb tide and burned. The canted hull of another seiner rests on the south shore, east of the mooring buoy.

As you make the passage, deer munching on kelp may keep a wary eye on you. A bear might amble along the shore, turning over rocks as it searches for food. Overhead a pair of eagles may ride a current. Fat ducks intent on escaping your boat will run along the water, wings beating frantically until, looking like overloaded seaplanes, they become airborne. Salmon may leap and splash, and seals surface for a quick look at your vessel. With luck, you might fall in astern of a homeward-bound fisherman and thus be piloted through, so you'll have a bit more time for wildlife watching.

Before mooring at Queen Charlotte City and picking up mail, doing the laundry, restocking the food locker and refueling, perhaps having a meal ashore, you may wish to land on the rocky west beach of Lina Island and search the tidal rocks for the three or more petroglyphs.

Moresby Island

BY CAR

Moresby Island is great for the boater, but for the hiker or motorist it has less to offer than Graham Island. It has fewer than 32 kilometers (20 miles) of public road, about half within Sandspit, the rest winding along Skidegate Inlet to the ferry ramp and to the separate water-taxi dock in Alliford Bay. Fewer beaches are accessible to drivers or hikers along Moresby's ragged and varied coastline.

In Sandspit, stop at Fletcher Challenge Canada Ltd's. Visitor Information Center during the summer, or their attractive office during other months, and pick up a free copy of "Forests for our Future," which includes a handy map of the company's main roads, and find out what roads the logging trucks are currently using. Phone: 637-5436.

During the summer a short film presentation is shown at the information center, and free bus tours of the logging area are scheduled. These popular, informative jaunts take 4 to 5 hours and provide opportunities for unusual photos. Bring your own lunch.

Fletcher Challenge, like most firms in the logging industry, is concerned with the environment, and offers information and this excursion to help you have a safe and pleasant visit to the islands — and avoid a head-on encounter with a gigantic truck barreling along with a 100-ton load of logs.

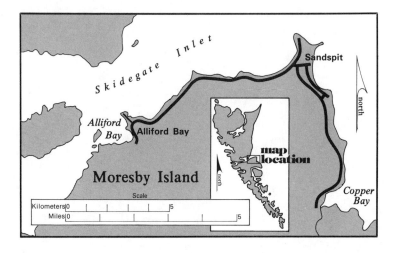

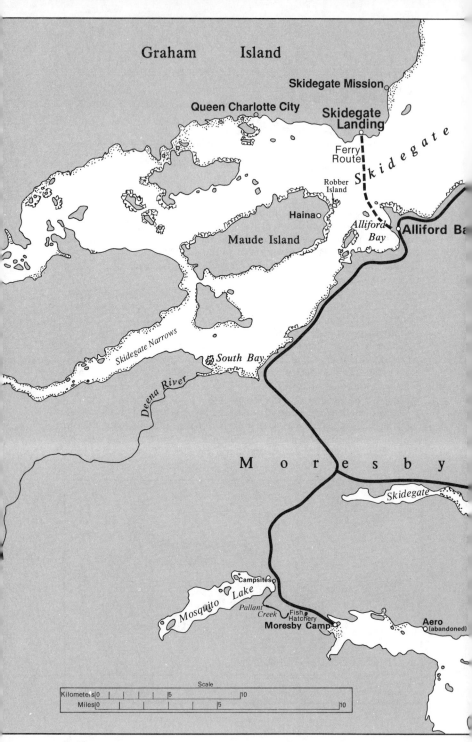

Graham Island

Skidegate Mission

Queen Charlotte City

Skidegate Landing

Ferry Route

Skidegate

Robber Island

Haina

Maude Island

Alliford Bay

Alliford Ba

Skidegate Narrows

South Bay

Deena River

M o r e s b y

Skidegate

Campsites

Mosquito Lake

Pallant Creek

Fish Hatchery

Moresby Camp

Aero
(abandoned)

Scale

Kilometers 0   5   10

Miles 0   5   10

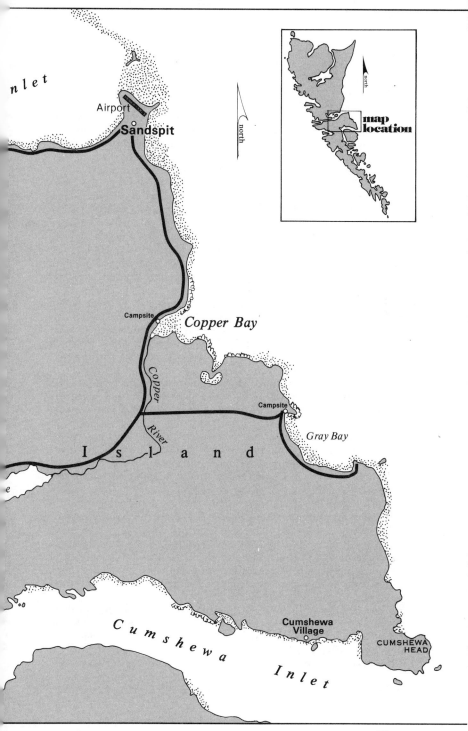

n l e t

Airport

Sandspit

north

map
location

north

Campsite

Copper Bay

Copper

River

I s l a n d

Campsite

Gray Bay

e

C u m s h e w a

**Cumshewa
Village**

**CUMSHEWA
HEAD**

I n l e t

Fletcher's Challenge's 11-kilometer (7 mile) private road between Sandspit and Copper Bay is always open to public use, and hundreds of kilometers of new and old logging roads may be used after working hours or on most weekends. But check at the office first. Main roads currently in use are usually well graded, though narrow. Roads in logged-off areas where a new crop of timber is growing are often rimmed with young alders; a few roads may have been blocked by a spring washout or a wind-felled tree. Some roads wend along broad valleys, often crossing clear trout or salmon streams. Branch roads climb to hillside camping spots overlooking tranquil lakes or to sheltered inlets surrounded by steep mountains.

A pleasant day can be spent on a road known locally as the Loop. Drive south from Sandspit, past the golf course and along the shores of Hecate Strait, where weathering drift logs create an obstacle course to the gravel beach. Proceed through stands of lush second-growth timber. Perhaps a pair of ravens will lead you along the road to shallow Copper Bay where, from August to October, salmon fishermen test their skill and luck. At the head of the bay are a number of modest cabins owned by Haidas from Graham Island and used when the Indians are engaged in catching their fish supply from April to November.

The gravel road follows the valley of the Copper River, often within sight of rushing water where a dedicated salmon, trout or steelhead fisherman may be seen. A sign at Spur 20 points to Gray Bay where 20 campsites have been dispersed along the bay's curved and sandy shores. Salmon are often caught here, from shore or from boats. A beach trail to Cumshewa Head starts at the road's end.

Another hiking trail of about a mile begins from Spur 29, marked with an information sign and a parking area. Picnic tables and toilets are provided. You may see a doe and fawn along here, or a spruce grouse and chicks.

Approaching Skidegate Lake you will see blackened logs, stumps and snags, some pointed skyward in weird configurations. This is the area where the Charlottes' most destructive fire of contemporary times took place. In the dry summer of 1957, after many acres of virgin timber were felled, a fire started and soon burned out of control, destroying thousands of dollars' worth of logs. Nature has reclaimed the land and a prolific growth of young trees nearly obscures the ebony remains. Birds and deer now thrive here.

A few kilometers beyond trout-filled Skidegate Lake is the Moresby turnoff, leading to Mosquito Lake, another favorite trout fishing spot, 11 campsites, a boat launching ramp and picnic site along the wooded shore. The lake was once used for log storage and sorting; deadheads now break the dark surface, perches for belted kingfishers.

Mosquito Lake was not named after those pesky insects, but for those versatile Mosquito bombers, fighters and reconnaissance planes of World War II, built in England, of spruce wood, much of it from here and other areas of the Charlottes.

From here the road continues to abandoned Moresby Camp, where there are 9 campsites, a small dock and a gravel boat-launch ramp on the shore of Cumshewa Inlet. You are now ready for excellent fishing, or exploring the sheltered east coast and its verdant, uninhabited islands.

Moresby Camp is as close as you can drive to the new South Moresby National Park. Its nearest border is some 50 kms (30 miles) away, accessible by air or water only. Hiking to the park is not feasible because of extremely rugged terrain.

A salmon hatchery, open to visitors, is operating along Pallant Creek, between Mosquito Lake and Moresby Camp. This is part of the federal government's multimillion-dollar Salmonoid Enhancement Program dedicated to doubling the current number of salmon within the next 15 to 20 years.

Leaving Moresby Camp and returning to the Loop, continue through the rolling, logged hills until dropping to near sea level at South Bay, Fletcher Challenge's log dump. During working hours, tiny, ultra-maneuverable boom boats charge wildly among the floating logs as the operators sort and corrall logs. A large crane is moored here and you might see a crew loading up to 2.5 million board feet of logs aboard massive self-dumping barges for towing to mills on the mainland.

The road, which often curves sharply, hugs the shore, then climbs into steep hills where deer and bear may be seen. Another road splits to the left, nearer the inlet, along the shore. Both branches bring you to Alliford Bay where large areas of concrete remain from an abandoned World War II RCAF seaplane base. From here patrols were launched to westward to help boats maintain a string of eight coastal watch stations. H & W Logging Company now uses this section of the bay and shore for booming and dry-land sorting.

While waiting for the ferry, or searching for rocks and small fossils, you might see the *Haida Monarch*, the world's largest self-loading, self-dumping, self-propelled log transport, loading up to 3.5 million board feet of timber.

The Haida Monarch *passing Balanced Rock, just northeast of Skidegate Mission, as she enters Skidegate Inlet to load. The* Haida Monarch *is the world's largest self-propelled, self-loading and self-dumping log transport.*

If you make any trip on a logging road, drive with your headlights on. You will be spotted sooner by the driver of a log truck as he hauls 100 tons of logs along a steep and narrow hillside road. Obtain permission before entering these roads; they are private. You may be told to wait and follow a logging truck. Encountering a logging truck could ruin your day.

Boats may be launched at Alliford Bay at the all-tides concrete ramp where the car ferry lands. Avoid conflict with the ferry's schedule. A pier and small float less than a kilometer north are used by water taxis.

Wave action often uncovers blue or red trade beads in the gravel beach at the abandoned Haida village of Haina, on Maude Island, where a school and church were once maintained. Gnarled apple trees and a solitary totem are all that remain of the village. At low tide go across the neck of land to Robber Island, where you will see the marble monument to Chief Gold Harbour — on which some long-forgotten carver misspelled *Chief*.

On a point at Maude Island's northeast edge are other Haida graves, some criminally desecrated by persons who removed or broke the marble gravestones.

BY BOAT
SKIDEGATE INLET TO LOUISE ISLAND

Again ready for the sea, enter Hecate Strait well north of the spit, avoiding the extensive and abrupt shoal north and east of Sandspit, where hull-smashing boulders lurk below the surface. Turning south, stay well clear of the coast, which is dotted with glacier-deposited rocks, until you pass Cumshewa Head.

Extensive beds of perennial kelp lie between Gray Point and Cumshewa

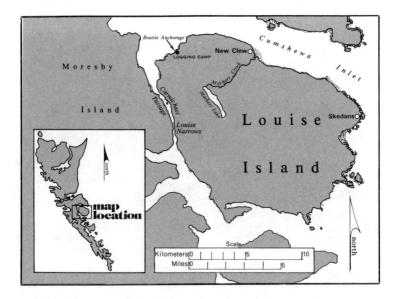

Derek Henry peers into a chiseled hole in one of the few standing totems at Skedans, an abandoned Haida village on the east side of Louise Island. Doric design on a portion of this mortuary pole is unusual.

Head — waiting to clog your engine cooling system, and snare propellers, oars, or paddles. Lost or discarded lines and fishing nets may also be concealed in the kelp, where your propeller is sure to find them. At high tide, kayakers may ride the quieter water between kelp beds and the stony shore.

At Cumshewa Village, an abandoned Indian settlement on the north shore of Cumshewa Inlet, old apple trees suggest early Indian contact with explorers, traders or sea otter hunters. Gray, cracked totems stare at large mounds of rocks. Do these rocks, well back from the beach, cover the remains of victims of smallpox or typhoid? Or are they just rocks that someone cleared from a hardscrabble garden before planting potatoes?

Along this sheltered east coast you may see weathered stumps, evidence of handlogging. Handloggers are hard-working people, usually a couple, who do selective logging. Each tree is felled close enough to the water's edge to get the log to salt water without the aid of land-traveling power equipment.

Skedans, an abandoned Haida village on Louise Island, is well worth seeing because it displays the Charlottes' second largest group of standing totems. The sea- and weather-wise Haidas selected practical and beautiful

Junction of old logging roads on Louise Island, near Mathers Creek. This road of sawn logs, made for trucks fitted with hard rubber tires, was much like a small railroad. This picture was taken in 1955. Today alder trees obscure this road and engulf the 16 old trucks abandoned nearby.

sites for their villages. Skedans is typical. The village was built on a neck of land with crescent beaches to north and south, where heavy dugouts might be launched or landed in nearly any weather. Kayakers and small-boat operators will usually find Skedans' south side best for landing or anchorage. Skedans is protected from northwest gales by a high cliff and surrounded by waters rich with lingcod, halibut and salmon. The rocks of the shore abound with abalone, rock scallops and edible mussels.

The totems include one with a 6-foot segment of Doric design, perhaps patterned after a sketch seen in a book owned by an early missionary. The "drums of Skedans" may be heard throbbing from a subterranean source when northeast seas pound into a small sea cave on the point.

A scale model of Skedans (formerly Koona), as it was at its height, is on display in the Royal British Columbia Museum in Victoria.

Skedans is one of our favorite villages. It is easily reached by small craft from Moresby Camp or Sandspit, on a day trip that may include stops at Cumshewa Village and New Clew before circling Louise Island and traversing Louise Narrows and Carmichael Passage. Prospective visitors should call at the Skidegate Band Council office and buy a visitor's permit.

The abandoned Indian village of New Clew is on the Louise Island side of Cumshewa Inlet. Near the village site, on the banks of Mathers Creek (once Church Creek), is a small graveyard with marble stones bearing inscriptions such as, "Kitty Kitsawa, she was a Methodist." What price, these carved markers shipped from Victoria? Did the seller demand a stack of prime pelts as tall as the monument?

Nearby, hidden by alders and a dense growth of prickly young spruce, stand old Leyland logging trucks with solid rubber tires. These trucks ran on a two-track trestled road made of logs sawn in half and laid smooth side up, with similar but lighter slabs as guides on the outer edges. Railroadlike turntables and Y-switches reversed the trucks' direction or shunted them to branch roads. Portions of this old road are hikeable, leading back to Mathers Lake at the head of a large valley logged off more than 50 years ago.

Mathers Creek provides excellent fishing for trout, steelhead and salmon. Take time to enjoy the beauty of this broad valley. New roads and branch roads have been constructed on Louise Island by the logging company now based on the shores of Beattie Anchorage, on the island's northwest side. Buoys offer safe moorage here near the booming and sorting grounds.

Scheduled flight service from Sandspit is maintained while the camp is operating.

Along Cumshewa Inlet and other coast bays and inlets, many of the lower hillsides are covered with uniform stands of the deep green second-growth timber that follows the logging done 10 to 75 years ago. Here, and in places like this, the crews often lived on float camps, a name derived from the log floats rafted to form compact, easily moved camps. Bunkhouses, shops, sheds and a cookhouse were built or skidded onto these sturdy floats. A camp was moored in a sheltered cove near a small stream until the area was logged off. Then the lines were cast off and the camp towed to a new location with a minimum of disruption and cost.

CUMSHEWA INLET TO SKINCUTTLE INLET

Continue westward in Cumshewa Inlet past a dilapidated pier at the derelict camp of Aero, on Moresby Island, once headquarters for the Charlottes' only railroad logging company. Moor alongside a small float at abandoned Moresby Camp. From August through mid-October, salmon fishermen often catch their limits in this area, near the head of Cumshewa Inlet or in adjacent streams.

In case you wish to return to Sandspit for supplies or mail, or one of your party has to catch a plane for home, you can often find a ride from Moresby Camp, or use your radio-telephone and call a taxi from Sandspit.

If you feel like a good hike, or have a four-wheel-drive vehicle, there's a rough road through a low pass and narrow valley to the shore of Peel Inlet, where it is possible to launch a boat.

Facilities are planned for Gordon Cove, on the south side of the head of Cumshewa Inlet, that include a boat launch, floats, additional mooring buoys and upgraded access road. These will make South Moresby National Park more accessible to seafarers.

All along Moresby Island's east coast, old buildings or teredo-eaten pilings record sites of former logging camps or canneries. The trash piles from those industries are now treasure troves for bottle collectors.

Scale
Kilometers |0 |5 |10 |20
Miles |0 |5 |10

north

H e c a t e

Tar Islands

Lost Islands

Lyell

Powriveo Bay

Island

Helmet
Island

Flower Pot
Island

Tanu

Takelly

Shu
Isl

Thurston
Harbour

Tanu
Island

Darwin

Hoya P.

Cumshewa Inlet

Louise Island

Sewell Inlet

Talunkwan
Island

Echo Harbour

BENT TREE
POINT

Klunkwoi
Bay

Carmichael Passage

Dana
Passage

Pacofi Bay

Crescent Inlet

Lockeport
(abandoned)

Anna Inlet

Anna Lake

Louise Narrows

Lagoon Inlet

Sewell Inlet

Pacofi Bay Settlement
(abandoned)

M   o   r   e   s   b   y

Aero○

Lagoon Bay
Cannery
(abandoned)

Sewell
(Moresby-Sewell)

Tasu Sound

Tasu○

Moresby Camp

Road to Sandspit

Newcombe Inlet

Pool Inlet

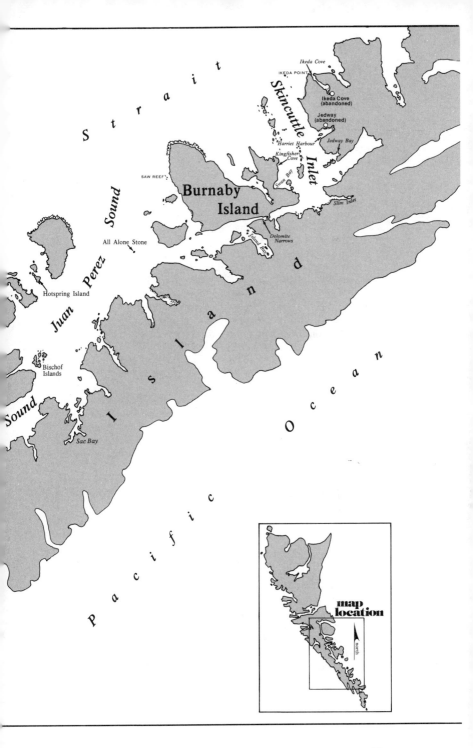

Strait

S

Ikeda Cove

IKEDA POINT

Ikeda Cove
(abandoned)

Skincuttle Inlet

Jedway
(abandoned)

Jedway Bay

Harriet Harbour

Kingfisher
Cove

SAW REEF

Burnaby
Island

Swan Bay

Slim Inlet

Juan Perez Sound

All Alone Stone

Dolomite
Narrows

Island Bay

I s l a n d

Hotspring Island

Bischof
Islands

Sound

Sac Bay

Pacific   Ocean

P a c i f i c

map
location

north

Anchoring in front of one of these places is a gamble, however, for the bottom is often littered with heavy cables or other discarded equipment.

Cruise through scenic and calm Carmichael Passage, a narrow gash between Louise and Moresby islands. The mountains that rise from these rocky, tree-covered shores have snow-covered peaks. Near the southern end of the passage, on the Louise Island side, are a buoy and log flat where fresh water can be obtained. The passage necks into Louise Narrows, a 40-foot-wide channel curving through the forest with leveelike gravel banks close to port and starboard. Catch this at high-water slack.

As the narrows opens, a small bay is sighted to the east. Westward is Lagoon Inlet, where an old cannery was converted into a logging camp and used for a short time before it partially burned. Trees have nearly reclaimed this site. The lagoon may be entered with a small boat at high-water slack through a constricted passage that is otherwise subject to tidal rapids. Salmon and trout streams drain to the sea through the extensive flats at the head, where black bears feed during the spawning season.

Cruising into Sewell Inlet, you will notice clearcut hillsides and hear high-powered diesel trucks. At the inlet's head is Sewell, a modern logging camp of about 20 persons and Queen Charlotte headquarters for the logging and tree farm operations of Western Forest Products Ltd. Floats for small craft and a ramp for amphibian planes are sheltered behind the log dump and booming grounds. A road about 10 kilometers (6 miles) long goes from Sewell to Newcombe Inlet on Tasu Sound, on the west coast of Moresby Island. A telephone is located in the camp office, and water may be obtained at the mooring float.

As you enter or leave Sewell, study the surrounding hillsides for examples of tree farming in its various stages. Near the shore is lush second-growth timber approximately 35 years old; above are trees hand-planted in a checkerboard pattern; farther up are patches of natural seeding, some hand-thinned; then the brown of freshly clearcut land; beyond, the mixed live and dead trees of an overmature forest.

Pacofi Bay boasts an excessively massive concrete seawall and a mysterious past. Built in 1910 by the son of one Count von Alvensleben, it was operated for only one year as a cold storage plant. In 1938, while a wrecking operation was going on at the site in preparation for new construction, an extensive concrete installation was discovered hidden under the old buildings. Experts concluded this might have been intended as a German submarine base. Today, only a tumbled two-story bunkhouse remains north of the seawall.

Along the east side of Dana Passage and almost overgrown by young alder trees are the remains of a beached and burned two-story float camp. The small bay usually affords protected anchorage.

A modern logging camp was in operation in Thurston Harbour on Talunkwan Island until late 1976, when logging was completed and the camp moved to Powrivco Bay, on Lyell Island. The hillsides are again green with a new crop. Steep gravel roads, now used by hikers or hunters, spiral into the glowering sky. Sunlight pierces the restless clouds, spotlighting the hillside, an eagles' nest, or the dark inlet where excited salmon leap from the chill water. Mooring buoys are located at the head of Thurston Harbour.

Excellent examples of the multilevel floors typical of large Haida community houses may be seen at Tanu, an abandoned Indian village on the east end of Tanu Island. Tired totems and crumbled longhouses arc around the protected landing beaches. Though uninhabited, this and the Charlottes' other abandoned Indian villages are on Haida reserves, owned by Haidas in Skidegate Mission or Haida. *It is unlawful to remove, harm or destroy any part of these old villages.*

Abandoned Lockeport sits at the entrance to tiny Anna Inlet in Klunkwoi Bay (Moresby Island). From 1907 to 1928 the fate of this settlement was tied to prospectors, mining claims, fishermen and canneries. Part of an old cedar shake trail still exists, climbing from the inlet to Anna Lake, a pleasant 20-minute hike. During the late 1960s the hills along Anna Inlet were drilled, cored and examined in hopes of making an ore strike. So far the attempt is just a repetition of an old story — more money going into the holes than coming out. Prospectors drilled in this region as recently as 1988. Establishment of the national park will probably end prospecting and mining within its boundaries. Yachtsmen will find sheltered anchorages in Anna Inlet.

Names on this area of the chart fire the imagination: Echo Harbour; Bent Tree Point; Crescent Inlet; Helmet, Flower Pot, Lost, Tar, Hotspring and Rainy islands; All Alone Stone; Saw Reef; Kingfisher Cove; Island Bay. Two other names, Powrivco Bay and Takelly Cove (on Lyell Island), were derived from the Powell River Company. a logging concern, and

This shell of a Haida longhouse which the Careys found on their first trip to the islands, in 1955, was at the abandoned Indian village of Tanu on Tanu Island. The longhouse has since collapsed. The house totem had been removed for preservation shortly before this photograph was taken.

T.A. Kelly, a colorful pioneer in the history of logging operations on the island. Until mid 1987 Frank Beban Logging Ltd. operated a modern camp in Powrivco Bay. The generous services once given will be greatly missed.

In 1955 we happened to stop at an old gold mine on the northeast side of Shuttle Island, located in the middle of Darwin Sound. On that particular day the three partners made the big decision to quit wasting the summer and their money on the mine. After demonstrating their method of operation they presented our bug-eyed 11- and 12-year-old sons with that day's gleanings — a few shiny flecks of dust, nearly a nickel's worth, placed, appropriately, in an aspirin bottle. The open shaft of that abandoned mine is easily found near a crumbling shack surrounded in summer by tall, bell-shaped foxglove.

DARWIN SOUND TO KUNGHIT ISLAND

Fresh water, clear and cold, is available from a hose secured to a deep-water float located in a small notch in Moresby Island and usually referred to as the water hole. It is west of Shuttle Island and entered from Hoya Passage. Mooring buoys are also located here.

Opposite the water hole is a small bay in Shuttle Island that power cruisers may enter — passing over a rock ledge — except at low tide. This gunk hole offers a secure anchorage, distinctive scenery above and underwater, and a central location for ranging out in the small boat to numerous beaches and seldom visited tiny coves.

Exploring the many bays, inlets, and islands in and around Juan Perez Sound might easily fill many happy days. With good charts and an alert bow lookout, you may navigate this fascinating area of rocks, islets, and islands where clear streams tumble from rolling, tree-covered hillsides. With a tidal stream of two to three knots, traversing four-mile-long Beresford Inlet — so narrow you may have difficulty turning your vessel around — is a unique experience.

The Bischof Islands, a serene group of one large and several small wooded islands and many drying rocks, forming a broken ring around a sheltered anchorage, are surrounded by feeding birds and marine life. Watch auklets and murrelets surface, tiny fish dangling from their beaks, then dive for more. Gulls ride drifting logs, whiling away the hours until the outgoing tide uncovers their next meal. You may be lucky enough to see a whale cavorting or just lazing across the sound.

An added pleasure while cruising along Moresby Island's east coast is obtaining enough salmon, lingcod, halibut, red snapper, abalone or rock scallops for at least one meal a day.

The sound can be uncomfortably rough during a southerly or easterly storm, but surrounding bays and inlets afford shelter for your craft, and many beaches for your crew to hike, though they accumulate less interesting ocean drift than outer shores due to their restricted entrances.

Late one summer, during only a few days in Juan Perez Sound, we saw over thirty immature eagles congregated here.

A soak at Hotspring Island is a must! The tub there used to be of Japanese design with heavy wooden planks and ample depth, unsheltered and encouraging a leisurely bath while enjoying an unimpeded view across Juan

Perez Sound. Now there are conventional tubs placed side by side, with an excellent view of the hot springs and sea. Another is modestly covered by a small shack of cedar and plastic. But enjoy the present. Mix the hot and warm running water and indulge in a steaming, slightly sulfurous, relaxing bath, without the discomfort of gradually cooling water, or enjoy the family-size hillside pool. In summer and during the salmon-seining and gill-netting season, you may have to await your turn while tired fishermen soak themselves. Wind and tide may abruptly change the sea conditions at your insecure anchorage on the southwest side of Hotspring Island. Buoys are located at nearby Ramsay Island.

There are more enticing little sandy beaches, bays and inlets along Moresby Island's east coast than you will have time to explore, even with a month's vacation. If it can't be a continuing project you should settle for touching the highlights of these seductive islands. In any case, a keen-eyed lookout is a must as you nose into some of these seldom explored coves and rock-encumbered passages, where a few uncharted rocks lurk.

After a rain, Sac Bay's dark waters — on the south side of rocky and baroque de la Beche Inlet — are brightened by mounds of foam riding seaward like icebergs from two chattering waterfalls. The shore is rimmed with black lichen-covered rocks, decorated with golden rockweed. On windless days the still water mirrors the steep hillside, surrounding your boat with trees that appear to be standing on their delicate tops.

Kat Island offers its short sand beach as a pleasant campground for kayakers. Eagles may watch from a nearby nest, and ever-curious seals will pop up to check on you.

No doubt you will enjoy some summer days so warm and still that sun-dried sand floats on the rising tide, and clam-shell halves are floated gently off the beach to drift away as tiny white coracles.

Interesting log or shake-covered cabins and lean-tos will be found along the quiet shores of Dolomite Narrows, Swan Bay and other isolated streams or beaches off the south side of Burnaby Island. These were built by young men and women trying to get away from it all; most have now been abandoned.

Over 120 years ago engineer Francis Poole and his crew drilled and prospected for copper in Skincuttle Inlet — without discovering anything of commercial value. You should find beauty in the Copper Islands, or enjoy tramping around Pelican or Poole points looking for one of Poole's hand-drilled adits.

Jedway, in Harriet Harbour, was born early in the 1900s and flourished as a center for prospectors until World War I. In 1961 it came back to life as an iron-mining town of more than 200 people. Iron concentrate was shipped to Japan from Jedway until mid-1968. The town was again laid to rest, the buildings razed or moved and an effort made to cover the scars of open-pit mining. Today the forest is rapidly reclaiming the site, creeping over washed-out roads and the area around the mine. The harbor here is subject to heavy squalls funneling out of the valley during strong southerly gales. At such times shelter can be found in nearby Jedway Bay, once site of a Japanese abalone cannery. A water hose and mooring buoy are at the head of the bay.

Scuba divers and snorkelers find their limit of abalone in the waters around Langara Island.

Waters around the Charlottes are unusually clear, increasing the pleasure and success of scuba divers or snorkel enthusiasts. Skincuttle Inlet encompasses over two dozen islands and islets with a variety of beaches. Its shoal waters, rich with spiny sea urchins, beche-de-mer, pinto abalone or rock scallops, are an excellent place to enjoy diving and snorkeling.

A wireless station was constructed on Ikeda Point in 1909 and operated until 1920. The roofless blue-green stone structure once housing a crew of radio operators is now hidden within the trees over half a century old but can be found by climbing the rocks on the point's south side.

Rusted narrow-gauge tracks, some dangling like rusting vines, lead from the shores of Ikeda Cove to an abandoned copper mine. In 1907 a Japanese fisherman-prospector opened the island's first profitable mine, shipping the ore to his home country.

The old sternwheeler *Dawson* was converted into a bunkhouse and moved here onto a grid of timbers and pilings, where her charred keel remains. Hikers may follow the old rail line through thick second-growth and blowdowns, or, climb uphill from the cove's head, ultimately striking a weathered gravel road twisting down from the open-pit mine to abandoned Jedway.

KUNGHIT ISLAND AND ST. JAMES ISLAND

From 1909 until World War II, Rose Harbour (named for a British politician) was a bustling whaling station employing 150 men. Wooden tanks rich with the smell of whale oil, tumbled buildings and remains of a pier once stood beside this all-weather bay. Mooring buoys are located close to shore. In springtime large daffodils cast a glow throughout the cleared area and in midsummer stalks of brilliant foxgloves brighten the clearing, where ruins mix with new imaginative buildings constructed by those who bought the old whaling station in 1978. Bits of whalebone and teeth, broken harpoon heads and a variety of bottles lie along the dark shore. It is a place of beauty and serenity.

The southeastern side of Kunghit Island is a series of four bays: Treat, Luxana, Howe and Woodruff, each with smooth sand beaches lapped by small waves and covered with accumulations of interesting drift. While attractive to visit, these open bays afford scant shelter and the nearly constant swell makes them uncomfortable overnight anchorages.

Exposed and rocky-shored Gilbert Bay gouges the southwest side of Kunghit Island. If the sea is quiet, you could anchor for a few hours in the half-mile-wide cove at the bay's northeast corner. Here, golden sands slope gently upward from turquoise waters, becoming rolling dunes covered with waving grass that retreats into the stunted forest. Driftwood decorates the storm-delineated high tide line. Japanese glass balls and other drift are tossed ashore by rows of breaking waves. Deer wander along the beach, nosing through the kelp, or stand quietly while munching on choice pieces.

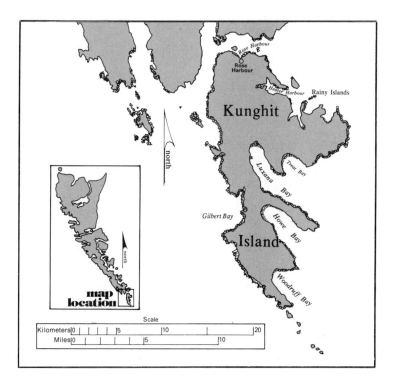

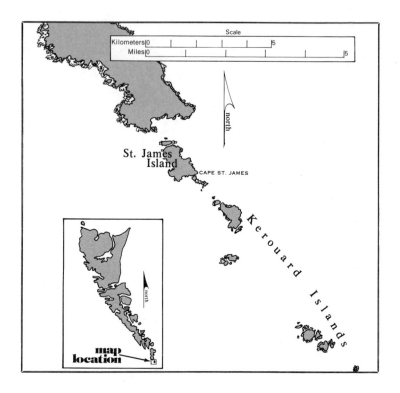

At St. James Island, it is a long climb up the steep metal ramp and past the helo pad to the top, where a light tower and meteorological building stand close together at Cape St. James. The view from the top is worth every step. From here the round-topped Kerouard Islands look like a string of elephants belly-deep in swirling water. These islands, with vertical cliffs on all sides, are breeding places for countless sea birds. Sea lions haul out and pup on some of the lower rocks. These ever-active waters are rich with food, attracting an abundance of fish, seals and sea lions and a vast variety of sea birds.

Current weather reports and forecasts are provided cheerfully by the three persons stationed at the cape, whose supplies, mail and relief personnel are brought in by helicopter. A walled area of sloping concrete the size of a tennis court serves as a catchment for water.

To telephone Cape St. James station for sea or wind conditions, call Vancouver (604) 662-0191 and you will be connected by way of Anek satellite.

A comfortable anchorage may be found midpoint on the east side of the drift-catching Gordon Islands. Sandy beaches and tidal pools filled with marine life attract photographers and beachcombers.

Top — *Betty Carey resting on a steep climb past the concrete catchment and tramway on St. James Island. At the top are a meteorological office and light tower.*
Above — *Sea lions haul out on ocean-washed rocks off the Charlottes' coast. About half of British Columbia's 5,000 sea lions feed and breed here.*

ANTHONY ISLAND TO GOWGAIA BAY

Unlike the gradually shoaling east coast, the west coast of Moresby Island is deep and its shore steep, often with almost vertical cliffs, and the 100-fathom curve lies little more than a mile offshore.

Remote, unsheltered bird-foot-shaped Anthony Island was the southwesternmost home of the Kunghit Haidas until abandoned around 1880. The nervous Pacific breaks on the rocky shore of this secluded 346-acre island. The village stood on a small east-facing bay. At high tide, small boats can enter the short channel through swaying kelp, and find a short, curved beach guarded by many totem poles. This is Ninstints, best preserved and loveliest of all the old Haida villages. Dugouts once struck out from here as Haidas set out to trade or fight with passing sailing ships, or to trade or do battle with mainland Indians.

Numerous trees have been removed, opening a view to the remaining poles, longhouse sites and village area. Brush and grass have been cleared, some leaning poles braced, and fallen poles raised above the damp ground. Gravel walkways lead among the totem poles. A small cabin has been built north of the old village, and in season, a park warden is in residence.

At low tide the canoe launching path, cleared perhaps two centuries ago, is still visible and usable, slippery with seaweed. Nearly hidden by encroaching forest are the tumbled and decaying longhouses whose shaped timbers still bear the scalloped cuts of an adz — perhaps an adz acquired in exchange for sea otter pelts during the voyage of Captain Dixon of the *Queen Charlotte*. Six grotesque, blackened poles record a major fire that occurred shortly before the dwindling Indian population moved to Skidegate Mission.

In 1958, Anthony Island was declared a Provincial Park so all might see the world's finest collection of standing Haida totems; remnants of a nearly lost civilization. This island received worldwide recognition when it was added to UNESCO's prestigious list of World Heritage Sites, in November 1981.

Louscoone Inlet (a mooring buoy is halfway along the east side) and Flamingo Inlet (Moresby Island) lure the beachcomber. These long, fjordlike waterways are natural catch-alls for a variety of Pacific drift. In addition, they are good salmon fishing. Sperm Bay in Flamingo Inlet is the last reasonable anchorage until you reach Gowgaia Bay.

On any of the island's three coasts, but particularly along the west side, gray, sperm and humpback whales can be sighted, spouting as they cruise along the outer rocks and reefs searching for food or passing during migration. You might even catch one of those rare moments when, in play or courtship, the great mammals leap clear of the sea, then fall with a resounding crash and flying spray.

A pod of killer whales — easily identified by their erect triangular dorsal fins — might sweep into an inlet looking for a meal. The 30-foot male has a dorsal fin that can be up to 6 feet high. At these times seals haul out onto the nearest rock or beach and it is possible to approach them within a few feet. The seals are willing to gamble on your intentions — they know instinctively the deadly intent of the killer whales. At other times a dozen or more Dall porpoise, up to 6 feet long and weighing 250 pounds, may suddenly appear alongside your boat, cavorting and splashing as they cross and recross the bow or glide under the keel, until they tire of the game and disappear as abruptly as they arrived.

Bones and carcasses of whales and porpoises are occasionally found along the Charlottes' shores. In 1971 my wife Betty claimed and skeletonized a 40-foot gray whale for educational use, and has sent skulls of the rare Stejneger and Cuvier beaked whales to the Royal British Columbia Museum in Victoria. Few beachcombers carry their avocation to this extreme.

On those days when the ocean is calm, you may sight Japanese glass net floats and bottles — even one carrying a message written in a foreign language. Sometimes one encounters long, sinuous paths of drift — gathered by the wind — containing kelp, limbs, logs, velella, jellyfish, bottles, and balls of glass or plastic.

If you are along the coast during the commercial halibut season, you might see a black-footed albatross gliding only inches above the rolling sea on wings that span nearly 7 feet.

You may see those largest of sea birds alight on the water, wings spread wide, feet like water skis, to feed on and quarrel over fish or squid. Getting airborne when the wind is light requires a long run and much flapping of the long, narrow wings. Or you may see the albatross's cousin, the sooty shearwater, which is about one-fourth as large. They, and screaming sea gulls, are searching for or feeding on red snappers or other fish discarded by the halibut crew.

The southwest end of Moresby Island is low and densely wooded. The headlands and shores of massive dark rock are usually devoid of any vegetation to 100 feet or more above sea level because of brutal, often sudden, Pacific storms that sometimes are churned up by winds well in excess of 100 knots. Sea birds, fish, shellfish and interesting debris can be found on the shores after these once- or twice-a-year events.

Late in October 1977, we witnessed one of the most savage and destructive of these storms. It commenced in the early forenoon. By noon the seas, driven by 75-knot winds, were breaking wildly across the entrance to Puffin Cove and crashing onto the inner beach. The winds continued to increase and the combers began to climb up and over the outer rocks, something we had never seen before. Gusts were sweeping water up from the lagoon and casting it about until I thought our cabin was inside a car wash.

Just before dusk, which came early, I saw what I would never have believed could happen. I thought I was watching a freak or rogue wave — I'd been hit by one of those years before while taking a tanker across the Gulf of Alaska one winter. I watched until I saw the wave again, then called Betty. The seas were striking one of the vertical outer rocks, racing up and over it, and continuing up another 100 feet — and that rock was 150 feet high! Those weren't rogues that day, just routine waves.

The wind continued to blow at a steady 125 knots and the storm lasted all night. The ebb tide couldn't escape the coast and remained about three feet higher than normal. By moonlight we watched those horrendous combers spill over the high rock all night.

Six days later the North Pacific calmed enough for us to head out for

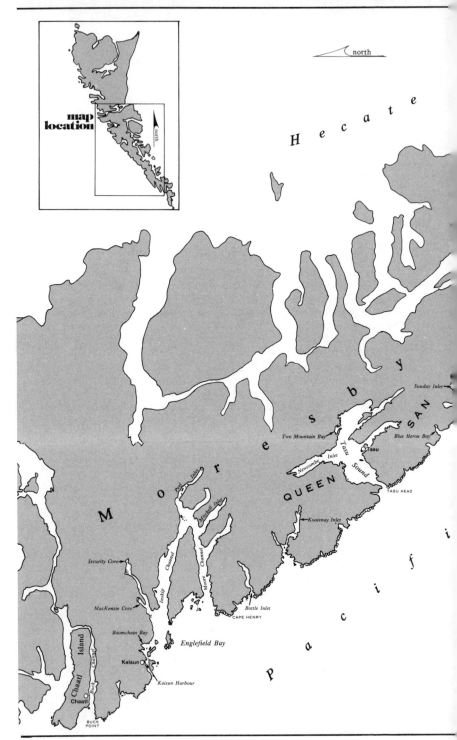

north

map location

H e c a t e

M o r e s b y

Sunday Inlet

Two Mountain Bay

Blue Heron Bay

Newcombe Inlet

Tasu

Tasu Sound

SAN

QUEEN

TASU HEAD

Kootenay Inlet

Peel Inlet

Mitchell Inlet

Security Cove

Inskip Channel

Moore Channel

Bottle Inlet

CAPE HENRY

MacKenzie Cove

Boomchain Bay

Englefield Bay

Kaisun

Kaisun Harbour

Chaatl Island

Buck Channel

Chaatl

BUCK POINT

P a c i f i

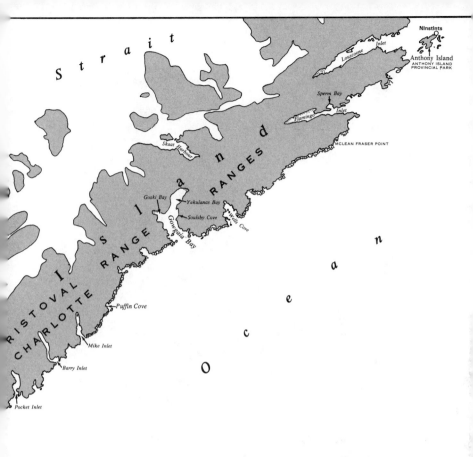

Precise boundaries of the South
Moresby National Park Reserve
had not been determined at
press time.

Scale

| Kilometers | 0 | | | | | 5 | | 10 | | | 20 |
| Miles | 0 | | | | | 5 | | 10 | |

Neil Carey looks at the grizzly bear mortuary pole at abandoned Ninstints village and wonders how much longer it will resist the ravages of age and gales. In 1955 the Careys admired more than three dozen poles rimming the gravel beach of this hauntingly beautiful and secluded site. Now, few more than a dozen stand.

Tasu. The ocean was covered with driftwood of all sizes and shapes, plus something new: storm-shredded wood chips. Bays were littered with floating logs. Other logs had been hurled into the forest. Glass balls? None. And the plastic floats we usually encounter after a storm must have been pulverized. Bottom fish and eels had been lifted from the ocean floor and hurled onto the shore.

Our experience has been that March and October are the fiercest months, but any month can produce a sudden storm of 60 knots or so.

Be alert for the tide rips that frequently occur off McLean Fraser Point. Isolated rocks lurk within a mile of shore. There are few beaches between

Nagas Point and Wells Cove that can be approached with safety.

Unsurveyed Wells Cove offers a wide assortment of beaches, sculptured rocks, crashing breakers, and gentle tidal streams. Perhaps an inquisitive deer, a sleek black bear, an imperious bald eagle or a playful seal will pose against those backgrounds.

At first glance Gowgaia Bay (often called Big Bay) may appear a fearsome mass of breaking seas and jagged reefs. However, it has been well surveyed and has a wide, deep entrance. Within are many kilometers of beaches as well as anchorages in Yakulanas Bay, Goski Bay and Soulsby Cove. But watch out; the wind at the anchorage can veer abruptly or pounce in violent gusts. Winds may strike a hillside and bounce back 180 degrees, the storm overhead moving in one direction, the surface winds in the opposite direction. Hikers might decide to check out the wooded lowlands between Yakulanas Bay and Skaat Harbour, on the east coast, or search for the World War II coast watch cabin and radio shack near the south side of the bay's entrance.

GOWGAIA BAY TO TASU

Tasu Sound and the six inlets between Gowgaia Bay and Englefield Bay have narrow entrances that are sometimes difficult to see. All are surrounded by steep mountains that after a rain are streaked with wispy falls. Throughout the islands, and especially on the craggy slopes of the west coast, a thin layer of soil nurtures an ever-growing weight of trees and shrubs; after extended rainfall or a jolting earthquake, there will be new landslides that leave great triangular scars and a jumble of broken trees at water's edge.

High bare peaks surround Mike, Barry and Pocket inlets where small streams tumble from hillsides wooded with wind-whipped spruce or cedar and deformed, shrub-size trees. All attract a variety of bird life. Usually these inlets are adequate anchorages, but when southeast gales blow they are subject to heavy squalls, or williwaws — sudden, violent gusts of wind moving down to the sea from coastal mountains.

At these times winds tumble down the steep hills, striking from all points, whipping up the sea and swirling water high into the air — a severe test for your ground tackle, and good reason for that second or third anchor plus extra line or chain. Find a notch alongside a vertical cliff and moor fore and aft to projecting trees or rocks, laying a kedge anchor to seaward and using the skiff as a fender between shore and boat. This is not a favorite method of mooring, but it is effective and will allow you to get some rest until the storm blows itself out in 4 to 36 hours.

North of Pocket Inlet limestone spires tower out of the sea. Behind a group of these spires is an inviting beach of golden sand where a rolling surf appears to tumble lazily and run up the beach. Study it a few minutes before making the landing; you might be able to avoid a dunking. Or you might choose to land on the rocks outside the surf line.

At the head of Sunday Inlet is a well-protected anchorage sheltered by high, treeless peaks of the San Christoval Range. The peaks are often covered until mid-September with glistening snow that melts just in time for them to receive a new coat in October or November. Deer, bears and

The author with the lower jawbone of a 50-foot sperm whale, the vertebra of a blue whale and a large Japanese glass float, all beachcombed on the west coast of Moresby Island.

a variety of waterfowl claim domain in the quiet inlet. Trollers often anchor here overnight between July and late September.

Two miles north of Sunday Inlet an open cove and a narrow rock-encumbered slot open into a leaf-shaped pocket named Blue Heron Bay. To the east, a clear stream drops in a series of falls from a water lily-ringed lake.

Mount de la Touche, one of the Charlottes' highest peaks (3,700 feet), rises midway between Tasu Sound and Sunday Inlet about one kilometer from the open sea. This is a typical winter scene, light snow on the peaks while the lowlands are snowfree. Note the scar of a landslide in the middle and the intrusion of black volcanic rock into the granite at the shoreline.

A remarkably beautiful view of the bay, ocean, lake and mountain peaks is gained by climbing the shelved gorge to its 500-foot-high summit. Bonsai-like trees, less than knee high, wrest a tenuous existence from fissures in the eroded rock, and tiny wild flowers add specks of color. Deer that never have seen a human being move nonchalantly out of one's path.

Sea lions often may be seen hauled out for a nap on sea-washed rocks midway between Blue Heron Bay and Tasu Head.

Three inlets and as many bays are hidden within Tasu Sound. Numerous gravel-bottomed streams in the area provide spawning beds for four species of salmon and abound with pools of hungry Dolly Varden and steelhead trout. Good sheltered anchorage can be found in Two Mountain Bay, where fist-sized fossils may be discovered in slatelike rock along the shore.

The company-owned mining town of Tasu closed in October, 1983. The buildings and a watchman remain. The facilities of this modern town, once home to some four hundred miners and their families, are no longer available. The economic contribution of the mine is greatly missed, for one half of the Charlottes' tax revenue originated here.

Tasu's original reason for being was an open-pit mine. In mid-1977 the operation shifted to underground mining. Since opening in 1965 the mine produced annually approximately one million tons of high-grade iron and copper concentrate for export, primarily to Japan. Trees and seeded grass are rapidly reclaiming the mine and townsite.

Fossil and pinto abalone shell found on a beach in Tasu Sound.

TASU TO SKIDEGATE CHANNEL

Five miles north of Tasu Sound is Portland Bay where the overflow from a small lake creates a lovely falls as it tumbles some 100 feet into the sea. There is no shelter here during any wind or sea.

Kootenay Inlet has not been completely surveyed. But those willing to chance it will be rewarded by beauty. The inlet is speckled with tree-covered islets, and there is a narrow but deep mile-long passage rimmed with overhanging trees which curves to suddenly reveal a large inner harbor. Low mountains surround the harbor and the game-filled valley at its head. A trail marked with bright tape has been made through the virgin forest

With hatches open to load iron concentrate destined for mills of Japan, an ore carrier lies alongside the wharf at Tasu. Begun as an open-pit mine, the operation moved underground, then closed in late 1983.

to intersect with a logging road to Sewell. Another interesting hike is along the dancing stream debouching in the northeast portion of the inlet; pass a tumbled log cabin, cross the stream and tramp through the ancient forest to other cabins and the adit of an old gold mine.

To the north of Kootenay knee-high salt grass edges the timbered flat lands at the end of narrow Bottle Inlet, where a meandering stream spills into the sea. In late summer the stream and the adjacent portion of the inlet are alive with pink salmon come home to spawn, attracting bears and eagles to do their own type of fishing.

Waters around Cape Henry and the entrance to Moore Channel move over an irregular shoal bottom creating, even in deep midchannel, high waves and a short chop when ebb tide and westerly winds meet.

East of Englefield Bay, in Moore and Inskip channels, you have a chance to explore five inlets without venturing into the open sea. One of these, Mitchell Inlet (Gold Harbour) was the scene, in 1851, of British Columbia's first gold rush. The gold was discovered by Haidas living on the west coast; later it was mined by men of the Hudson's Bay Company, who began to worry when American ships arrived with prospectors from California gold fields. The HMS *Thetis* was ordered into the area to proclaim British sovereignty. Her crew was kept busy surveying and assigning names. Soon the small lode was extracted, and ever-hopeful prospectors rushed off to the Fraser River or Cariboo strikes. It is still interesting to fossick around the old mine and get a few pictures of a small ore crusher rusting in its tumbled shelter.

Excellent fresh water may be obtained from a hose secured to a stiffleg and mooring buoy at the head of Douglas Inlet — courtesy of the crew of the Fisheries Patrol Vessel *Sooke Post.* Pay attention to the weather, because if a northwester is blowing, it will funnel up the inlet, producing whitecaps around the buoy.

A logging company operated in Peel Inlet from the mid-60s to 1970, leaving a leveled camp area and a rough hillside road still used by vehicles with four-wheel drive, and hikers to pass through a valley to Moresby Camp in Cumshewa Inlet.

As you head seaward through Inskip Channel, toss a weighted lure over the side and slow down a bit to troll for salmon, or stop and jig for halibut and lingcod. It shouldn't take long to catch the main course for your next meal.

Instead of rolling all night in Kaisun Harbour or Boomchain Bay, anchor in Security Cove or in a bight along the south side of Security Inlet. Set your crab trap anywhere on the grassy, shallow bottom near a stream. Or fish in the two fine salmon and trout streams that meander through magnificent stands of virgin timber before pouring into the cove. Deer often frolic along the shore, only to glide into the shadows of lichen-draped spruce trees when you approach in a skiff. The small cabin on the north side of the cove is owned by the Department of Fisheries.

Tiny unsurveyed MacKenzie Cove has been the subject of hopeful study and test drilling by crews of prospectors, all of them intrigued by large deposits of limestone and all evidently finding nothing of commercial value. The remains of temporary cabins and plastic shelters are just inside the forest.

A single totem stands above the gravel shore of the abandoned Indian village of Kaisun, where a landslide has covered part of the old village site. This kelp-encumbered and rolling anchorage is surrounded by islands, some with small caves waiting to be explored.

Although Kitgoro Inlet has not been properly surveyed, it may be, at other than low tide, entered with caution through a narrow, shallow, and kelp-choked entrance. We have obtained shelter here, in deep water — anchored and tied to the trees — on the northwest side during a westerly storm of over 80 knots.

Tiderips often occur off Buck Point's bold and worn rocks near the southern entrance to Buck Channel, leading to Chaatl, an abandoned Indian village on the southwest side of Chaatl Island. Only two totems remain standing, keeping company with the spirits of Haidas. The better totem hides amidst the trees some 500 yards east of the main village site. Some refer to one of its carved figures as a spider. To me, it looks like a mosquito. The venerable hereditary chief of Chaatl once told my wife what it was like to be a boy in that village when most of its inhabitants were dead or dying of smallpox: "I had no one to play with." What a poignant memory and succinct statement of tragedy.

At the head of Buck Channel is Canoe Pass, a winding connection to Armentieres Channel. At low tides the pass dries at the east end. It begins to cover when the tide tables predict 6 feet of water at the Tofino reference station. Those with small boats and local knowledge often use this pass.

From Chaatl Island you return through Skidegate Channel to the starting point of your Moresby Island cruise.

An old island saying goes, "If you don't like the weather, wait five minutes and it'll change." The Charlottes are notable for other kinds of change, too, with attendant fluctuations in population. In 1835 there were about 6,000 Haidas scattered over the islands. By 1900 fewer than 1,000 people — Haidas and white settlers combined — could be found. Today there are some 6,000 inhabitants. Each year a few new families arrive; others depart. It is too soon to speculate on changing employment patterns generated by creation of the South Moresby National Park Reserve. In logging, 110 loggers plus support personnel lost year-round jobs. Many families have had to leave the Charlottes and seek jobs elsewhere. Will other families come, attracted by the hope of serving tourists in this short-season, undeveloped and expensive-to-visit area?

It is not unusual for a new town or camp to materialize in a previously uninhabited place. During the 1960s, Tasu and Jedway sprang into existence. Then Jedway vanished after only seven years — and now Tasu has closed. Each summer one or more mineral or oil exploration crews quietly prospect these islands. Loggers move in, build roads, clear-cut large patches of the forest, replant some of the land, then move on to new sites. Logs and fish are the Charlottes' great renewable resources. Businesses open; some prosper, others fold. Schedules are made, then ignored or canceled. There will always be hope, dreams, frustrations and changes in the enticing Queen Charlotte Islands.

Possibly after reading this you have concluded that the seagoing aspects of the Charlottes have been overstressed. But all islands are water-oriented. Everyone and everything moving in or out of the Charlottes has to pass over or through the surrounding seas, the primary route of transportation and a place of employment, a source of food, and areas of recreation. The sea's moderating influence here eliminates extremes of summer or winter, thus making the islands different from the mainland. Of all the Charlottes' settlements or camps only the logging camp at Eden Lake is not alongside salt water.

As mentioned before, no one should try to squeeze a visit to the Charlottes into an inflexible schedule. Flexibility is imperative for those traveling by sea, where adequate time is often synonymous with safety.

Although not prepared for a great invasion of tourists or prospective residents, the Queen Charlotte Islands are definitely a rewarding, off-the-beaten-track part of the world to see and to enjoy.

SOUTH MORESBY NATIONAL PARK RESERVE

Agitation for the establishment of a park on South Moresby Island began more than a decade ago. Few locals took the idea seriously. The need for employment, the demand for forest products, the tax potential for all levels of government, and the fact that trees are a renewable resource — especially

Visitors at the end of their trip display some of their souvenirs, beach-combed on the islands' west coast. In addition to glass fishing floats from Japan, the family took home shells, a bamboo pole from the Orient, an eagle feather, and bottles — including one with a message dropped from a foreign ship.

fast-growing in the Charlottes — were taken for granted. Besides, large areas of South Moresby had been logged as early as World War I.

There were acrimonious arguments, propaganda, letter-writing campaigns, protests, even civil disobedience and events staged for the media — more interested in confrontation, it sometimes seemed, than in objective reporting.

Someone coined the term "Galapagos of the North." Not an apt term considering that Europeans had been here for two hundred years, and had introduced deer, elk, beaver, muskrats, squirrels, raccoons and (inadvertently) rats, plus livestock and assorted plants. And how about the Haidas, resident here for thousands of years? And who were those, before the Haidas, who carved the petroglyphs?

The Haidas discovered gold in Mitchell Inlet; it was mined by Hudson's Bay Company employees in 1851. Mining, logging, commercial fishing and seafood canning became the economic base.

In short, the Charlottes are far from being an untouched wilderness awaiting scientific study.

The loggers continued to log. Hand-planting of seedlings was greatly increased. Thinning of new growth began. The word "silviculture" entered the vocabulary of the islands. Some second-growth areas were harvested, sons logging where their fathers or grandfathers bent over crosscut saws.

The provincial government issued cutting permits. Protests were organized. Cutting permits were revoked. The camp on Lyell Island was closed. Single men flew off-island. Families stayed and school continued. Loggers went on UIC (Unemployment Compensation Insurance). Cutting permits were reissued. Camp reopened. Loggers flew back to Lyell. More protests. Then a few Haidas, some in native regalia including button blankets — they looked great on late TV evening news — went to Lyell, blocked the logging roads and claimed the Queen Charlotte Islands as their own. Some Haidas were arrested. More media coverage.

The media ignored the unemployed Haidas and other Natives who had worked in the logging camps. "And they're damn good loggers," says Sandspit resident Cliff McInnis, retired bull-bucker who has logged up and down the B.C. Coast.

In July, 1987, a memorandum of understanding was signed by the federal and the provincial governments stating that a South Moresby National Park Reserve would be created. (How about those Haida land claims?) The camp and settlement of the Frank Beban Logging Co., at Powrivco Bay on Lyell Island, was shut down (and Frank Beban, target of the anti-logging faction for more than a decade, died on Lyell of a heart attack at age 47).

The memorandum of understanding included $106 million for compensation and development. Immediately unemployed loggers at Lyell were paid compensation. Loggers laid off at Sewell in October, 1988, were not, though their employment was ended by the reduction in size of Tree Farm License 24 by creation of the park. Displaced families looked for new jobs and homes. The school closed. The community of Sewell became history. The small camp will operate about 150 days a year instead of year-round.

Tourists of 1988 couldn't get to South Moresby in the family car or RV, and they never will be able to. Many chose to drive to Graham Island and see Naikoon Provincial Park, and any other place they could reach by road or a short trail. Some chartered boats, planes or helicopters. Others who brought or rented kayaks paddled off to adventure. A few slipped car-top or trailered boats into the salt chuck and headed south, fishing, exploring and camping ashore. They returned tanned and happy.

The park agreement was finally signed in July, 1988. Park officials opened an office in Queen Charlotte City and are working to make this a great tourist destination. They need the support and help of all of us who live here and, of course, input from you tourists.

At present there are no search and rescue teams in South Moresby, nor camps with medical, repair, supply, communication nor shelter facilities. You are on your own. If you think you'll need it, bring it. In summer you should see boaters and probably a passing plane or helicopter. Attracting attention is the problem. Movement, reflection, silhouette, contrast may help. Three of anything — fires, shots, flashes — is a standard distress signal.

Late one summer Betty and I picked up a lone hiker, overdue because of foul weather and much more rugged topography than the maps indicated. He attracted our attention with light from the flash unit of his camera. "Have about 40 more flashes, I think," he told us. Wisely, he had left a time schedule with his girlfriend, who got the search going. (She is now his wife.)

Tell some reliable person where you're going and when you expect to return. A pocket-size VHF marine radio is good emergency equipment and it gets you the weather reports. Floater coats or suits, distress flares and dye markers are almost as necessary as a sharp knife, waterproof matches and a pocket compass.

The memorandum of agreement includes a $50 million Queen Charlotte Island development fund, to upgrade tourist facilities and help ease the islanders through the transition from logging to tourism.

The Haidas, who claim the Charlottes, do not want any of the $50 million spent until they have an agreement with the federal government about their part in planning and managing the park. Their elected chief says the park will be closed to general tourist traffic next year if no agreement is reached. Not quite the happy picture envisioned when the park was established.

I include this background information so you will not be shocked when you meet a resident who is not quite so enthusiastic about the park as you are. Remember, the price has been high for many who live, or once lived, on Moresby Island.

A small-boat harbor is promised for Sandspit — a facility needed long before the park became an idea. But now Sandspit's population has decreased by one-fourth as householders have been forced to sell at depressed prices and leave. Businesses have closed.

And headquarters for the South Moresby National Park? They're on Graham Island.

Adjustments will be made eventually; problems will be solved; but there's no need to wait. However you travel and whatever your budget, you will find the Charlottes a rewarding experience and a place to come back to.

CHANNELS FREQUENTLY USED IN MARITIME MOBILE SERVICE

STATION FREQUENCIES

PURPOSE	SHIP	COAST	VHF CHANNELS
Distress, Urgency, Safety, and Calling.	156.8 MHz 2182 kHz 500 kHz	156.8 MHz 2182 kHz 500 kHz	16
Continuous Weather. **Weather, Traffic List** **and Notships.**	 2054 kHz	*161.65 *162.55 *162.40 **2054 kHz	21B WX1 WX2
Ship and Coast Guard **Public Correspondence.**	157.3 157.225 2054 kHz 2340 kHz	161.9 161.825 2054 kHz 2458 kHz	26 84

*continuous broadcast

**broadcast at scheduled times

Index

**Many other fascinating books are available from
ALASKA NORTHWEST.
Ask for them at your favorite bookstore,
or write us for a free catalog!**

ALASKA NORTHWEST BOOKS™
A Division of GTE Discovery Publications, Inc.
130 Second Avenue South
Edmonds, Washington 98020

Or call toll-free 1-800-331-3510